DISCOVERING

TREASURES

OF

PEACE

DISCOVERING

TREASURES

OF

PEACE

by Mary Gemming, Ph.D.

ABOUT THE BOOK

The purpose of this book is two-fold:

1) To understand how to fully utilize your inner power so that you can rise to a higher quality of existence;

2) To comfort those who have had their share of life's struggles. You will learn how to calm hurt and confusion and find the spiritual light in order to spend the rest of your days surrounded by gentle love and peace.

"Mary's first book, <u>Mystical Secrets of the Stars</u> was so inspirational. Now we have <u>Discovering Treasures of Peace</u> which will surely help many people achieve peace and joy."
    -Esther Gordon, CEO, Eden Literary Agency.

This book is dedicated to those precious souls who have sacrificed a great deal in order to bring these teachings to humanity.

Contents

Foreword xi

Prologue xiii

Section One: Tapping Your Inner Power 1
Treasure Number One: *Developing Your Intuitive Power* 3
Clairsentience 5
Clairvoyance 6
Clairaudience 7
Telepathy 7
Psychometry 8
Centering: Attuning To Your Inner Power 11
Summary 14
Treasure Number Two: *Making Decisions Easier* 17
Pendulum Exercise 17
The Power Of Dreams To Make A Decision 20
Dream Incubation 21
Dream Journal Outline 22
Visualization Technique 23
Summary 26

Section Two: Creating Inner Peace 27
Treasure Number Three: *PRAYER* 29
What Is The Source Of Contentment? 30
The Dynamic Power Of Prayer 31
A Miraculous Healing Through Prayer 33
Prayer Steps That Never Fail 35
A Final Thought From A Well-Known Expert On Prayer 39
Treasure Number Four: *Meditation* 41
Breathing Exercise 41
The Protection Exercise 42
A Meditation Exercise 44
Treasure Number Five: *Contemplation* 49
Sunshine Exercise 50

Section Summary..54

Section Three: Making Your Home A Haven Of Peace 57
Treasure Number Six: *Improving Your Surroundings* 59
Cleansing Your Home 60
Feng Shui 61
Colors 63
Music..65
Candles And Aromatherapy...65
Pictures And Decorations..68
Flowers And Plants..69
Setting Up A Sacred Place 70
Treasure Number Seven: *Personal Relationships*...............................73
Transmuting Violet Flame Decree 75
Forgiveness Affirmation 77
Law Of Forgiveness Decree 78
Sacred Half-Hour Exercise..78
Section Summary..79

Section Four: Bringing Peace Into Your Workplace 81
Treasure Number Eight: *Improving Relationships With Colleagues* 83
Associative/Free Form Writing 86
Angel Of Peace Exercise 88
Harmony Exercise 89
Treasure Number Nine: *Making Physical Adjustments*
In The Work Atmosphere 91
More Feng Shui 91
Crystal Power...92
Crystal Exercise...96
Laughter To The Rescue 97
Section Summary..99
Epilogue: *A New Era*..101

FOREWORD

This book is totally suitable for beginners seeking knowledge of that illusive, interior "other world" which seems just beyond our grasp. While most of us are immersed in a world of exterior facts, bringing a sense of discontentment, we are led into a type of self-seeking that lacks a permanent satisfaction.

I see humanity as living in two worlds: the objective or exterior world and the subjective or interior world. In the exterior world we have been taught that we are separate, cut off from all other souls. But in the subjective, or subtle interior world we are all connected.

The exterior world is a mortal world of finite things that are born and die. Often we believe this is the only world we share—but at some point we intuit the subtle world of the soul which is interior to all living things—from plants to animals to humans.

The interior immortal world can open to us a perceptible presence of immortal soul bodies of harmonic resonance. And here is where we get to know what I call the "experiencer within." We may be out of harmony with people and situations in the exterior world; yet in the interior world we can transcend any disharmony and experience our oneness, our connectedness and find peace.

This book can help us to reconnect our parts of being.

Consciousness divides into three parts called conscious, subconscious, and unconscious or superconscious. These parts or states of consciousness are divided by differing rates of vibration, ranging from low, middle and high.

We can get these parts of our being to resonate in harmony with each other by using the techniques put forth in this book.

Enid Hoffman, Sarasota, Florida, May 11, 1999

Enid is author of *Huna;A Beginner's Guide, Develop your Psychic Skills, Expand Your Psychic Skills, Hands; A Complete Guide to Palmistry.* Her books have sold thousands of copies and are still in print.

(Enid passed into spirit at midnight, January 2, 2000. She will be fondly remembered by those of us who were privileged to enjoy her lively friendship.)

PROLOGUE

When I was a little girl, my mother took me along on visits to her friend Dora. I was fascinated by this old woman, who seemed so exotic with olive skin and blue eyes that sparkled when I called her my adopted grandmother. A closeness developed between us as she captured my interest with her stories.

Dora had been born in the late 1800's, when many children were delivered at home instead of in hospitals. She told us that she had been born with "the veil," which was extremely out of the ordinary.

The veil was a piece of membrane that covered a newborn's eyes and was believed to indicate the gift of clairvoyance. According to Dora, most midwives were aware of the phenomenon of the veil and were supposed to remove it carefully, with respect for the natural gift it portended. The veil was to be put in a place for safekeeping; otherwise, the infant would be cursed with bad luck.

Apparently Dora's mother threw the veil away, because Dora had more than her share of trouble and misery. She learned many years later that she was a "love child," conceived during an illicit love affair. As she grew up, she was treated cruelly by her mother, who secretly agonized about her infidelity every time she set eyes on her daughter.

When Dora was seventeen years old, she fell in love with a young man who adored her. While they were eloping to another state, her mother called the police, who found her and brought her home. Dora's parents forced her to marry an older man, and she suffered for many years in this loveless match.

I was staggered by Dora's clairvoyant abilities. Many times she would describe events she had "seen," and then days, months, or even years later, the incidents would unfold exactly as she had predicted.

One day she told my mother and me about a second marriage in my mother's future. Dora predicted that Mother would marry a man who would be a prosperous widower. We were puzzled upon hearing this, because my father was in good health. But true to Dora's word, he passed away several years later, and Mom married a widower with whom she was able to travel and enjoy material comfort.

When I was a teenager, Dora predicted that I would take a job in California and do extensive traveling. This baffled me, because I had no aspirations in this direction. Yet, this did come true.

Astounding information was revealed at Dora's cozy Cape Cod home. One day when I was enjoying a cup of tea and the aroma of her baked bread, I looked up to notice her staring at me from across the kitchen table. I asked if something was wrong, and she answered no.

"I am looking at a huge angel standing in back of you," Dora explained. "She has a message for you. She says she is called an Angel of Power. Angels of Power teach how to release the spiritual energy latent within each soul."

"What?" I asked with great surprise.

"Her name is Sophiel," Dora went on. "Because you have shown a desire for deeper levels of knowledge, she has come to help you with your spiritual quest. If you think about her while you are alone, you will be able to sense her presence. And she will guide you to books that will enhance your learning."

"What does she look like?" I asked, still in something of a daze.

"She has a sky-blue robe and blonde hair." Dora stopped for a moment to pause. "See the tremendous vibration, through the blue radiation which forms her energy."

I tried to envision all that Dora described. Truthfully, this was too overwhelming for me to grasp at that time.

I wanted to know more, but Dora was finished. I knew from experience how she expressed her visions: She suddenly blurted out what she was seeing, then would not talk about it afterwards. One day, feeling frustrated for details, I asked her why.

"I'm afraid," she confessed. "A minister told me we are not supposed to know what the future holds. Predicting the future is the work of the devil and can put you in hell, he said."

Dora's eyes darkened, and her face became tight and etched with tension.

My fascination with clairvoyance did not end with that last statement. In fact, it sparked more fire to my curiosity.

Having shown me that more existed than what the physical eyes could see, Dora continued to have a profound influence on me and my life. Besides, I was beginning to have clairvoyant experiences myself. I dared to follow a path of study which evoked some ridicule from relatives. Any interest in, or study of, the so-called "supernormal" was highly criticized at that time--while it is widely accepted today. I was determined not to let limiting taboos keep me from understanding what was taking place within me.

I questioned the minister's statement that insight into the future could put you in hell, because Dora's guidance helped me during my confusing teenage years. Then, later on, an inner guidance steered me through tricky situations.

I still remember the anxiety on Dora's beloved, wrinkled face when she repeated the minister's warning, and I think, "How sad that a woman who possessed such wondrous gifts was made to fear them! *How tragic that her special abilities evoked guilt that crippled her spiritual knowledge and potential!* "

Fortunately, since 1986, society's attitude toward spiritual matters has shifted. One example: At noon Greenwich time, December 31, 1986, millions of men and women participated in a global event called World Healing Day. It was a grass roots effort, initiated by John Randolph Price of The Quartus Foundation, to spend one hour praying for peace, love, and understanding in a simultaneous global mind-link. It was a beginning toward restoring the world to sanity and upliftment. This effort continues each year on December 31, as participation keeps growing.

Instead of shrinking from our gifts of prophecy or healing, and giving our personal power to others who would like to control us, we are beginning to cultivate these gifts within ourselves, and, as a result, growing spiritually. We are on an upward spiral in consciousness. We are learning how to shift our perception from the ego to the heart.

WHY NOW?

Why is this happening now? Why are mainstream national news magazines offering cover stories about the quest for the spiritual? Why are spiritual study groups meeting in homes across the country to explore inner growth and peace? Why are books about the spiritual path climbing the best-seller lists and staying there for months? Why are television stories about angels sending the ratings skyrocketing? Why is our mass consciousness expanding?

The answer is not such a mystery: The universe is expanding, and we are part of the universe. As we expand in consciousness, new manifestations of right brain activity occur. Intuition is one of those activities. Consequently, we need to understand the different forms in which intuition occurs, as you will see in Section One. By learning how to tap into this inner power, we are guided out of confusion and assisted in making the right decisions.

Through the faculty of intuition we can penetrate the veil of darkness which had shut down the communication between humanity and the Ascended Masters (Saints) and Angelic Hosts of heaven. New realization of the angelic world is illuminating the consciousness of human beings. Where there was darkness, a new light is dawning.

We are entering the Age of Spiritual Freedom. What does that mean? It means overcoming all limiting or discordant conditions and promoting an environment in which to learn who and what we truly are. It means freedom from fear. It means having the ability to see beyond appearances. It means feeling protected from within and without through the power of Divine

Love and Light. And this power will give us faith and hope to overcome anything that threatens our welfare.

Prior to every millennium, an influx of information empowers humanity to prepare for the new energies that will pour in. If our minds are open to receive this essential knowledge, it can turn lives around. This is why angels are appearing to humans. Angels are energies. They are bringing their energies to earth to uplift humanity. <u>Guideposts</u> publishes a magazine called <u>Angels on Earth,</u> containing inspirational stories about angels saving and healing lives.

The average person is focused on outer concerns such as work or relationships, rather than inner power, which needs to be awakened. In some people, it *is* being awakened, but because of their lack of knowledge, they do not understand what is taking place.

The purpose of this book is twofold:

1) To help you understand how to fully utilize your inner power so that you can rise to a higher quality of existence. You will be taking steps across a bridge that leads to spiritual awakening and empowerment;

2) To comfort those who, like Dora, have had their share of life's struggles. But unlike Dora, you will learn how to calm your hurt and confusion and find the spiritual light, so you may spend the rest of your days surrounded by gentle love and peace.

I have outlined sections for creating peace in your inner world (through intuition, prayer, meditation, attunement to God and self) and your outer environment (workplace, home and dealings with other people) to help you achieve a special balance.

These sections will help you to move toward a peaceful existence by creating calm environments from the inside out. You will begin to treasure your life and feel protected within the atmosphere you create.

The first section will awaken your intuition in a "fun" way, learning to interpret and trust the messages you receive and marvel at the way they help you in daily circumstances.

The second section will build a steady center within you through prayer, meditation and contemplation. Once that core of peace is felt, we will turn our attention to improving the physical environment—your living space and workplace.

Sections three and four will teach you how to apply spiritual principles to the outer world to bring tranquility into your home and office.

Using lessons and exercises that I have gathered in several years as a spiritual teacher and advisor, you will transform your relationships with family, friends, and co-workers into more accepting, loving and joyful interactions. These are easy, practical instructions which will enable you to surround yourself with peace both inside and out.

I invite you to begin a journey toward discovering the treasures of peace. It is a short path, but it is an excursion that will change your life forever. Let us begin as if we are strolling along a beach where we encounter a treasure chest. Are we looking at Blackbeard's lost treasure? Or is it the legendary treasure of *El Dorado,* "The Golden One?"

Take a look within to discover the value of each treasure tucked inside.

SECTION ONE: TAPPING YOUR INNER POWER

TREASURE NUMBER ONE: *DEVELOPING YOUR INTUITIVE POWER*

"Be still and know I am God."
-Psalms, 46:10

"Will you marry me?"

Ken asked me the question I had dreamed of hearing after dating him for eleven months. But instead of being elated, something strange happened. An eerie, invisible force was pushing on my chest! I felt a jolt so strong that Ken's arms dropped away from my shoulders. A terrible feeling came over me. I noticed a startled look on Ken's face. He was experiencing something, too, and must have been as astonished as I was.

Many moments went by as we sat in his car in front of my house trying to understand what was happening. At eighteen, I didn't know what to do. Finally, this handsome young man said in a puzzled voice, "What's wrong, don't you want to marry me?"

Still dumbfounded, all I could say was, "I-I don't know." My thoughts were not clear. Only one thing was certain: My answer was not supposed to be yes. But it did not make sense at the time. I was nuts about Ken! He was charming and a lot of fun. We seemed compatible. I knew I was in love with him. However, I had an inner feeling that something was wrong.

After that night, our relationship became awkward and unhappy. We would break up, then get back together. We really cared about each other, but a continuing feeling of uneasiness ultimately drove us apart.

A few years later, I heard that Ken had gotten married. Shortly thereafter, I read in the newspaper that he had been arrested for beating his wife. This turned up several times in the newspapers. I found out that he had cheated on her, too. In the end, it became obvious that I had been protected from physical abuse and marital infidelity by following an inner faculty.

If you think about it, a similar phenomenon may have happened to you. A "hunch" or "gut feeling" will come over you to strongly guide you toward one path, or away from another. Sometimes the messages come seemingly at random. They can apply to a future event, or, as with my response to Ken's proposal, to something that is happening right at that moment. What inner faculty makes it possible to receive these messages? The most accurate word for it is intuition. Some individuals call intuition a "sixth sense" because it goes beyond the realm of the five physical senses.

What is intuition? The American College Dictionary defines it as a "direct perception of truths...independent of any reasoning process." That is a good formal definition to satisfy the rational thinkers out there, but I have to say that intuition is much more than that. To me, intuition is a sacred key that unlocks the door to higher levels of knowledge and consciousness.

The highest level of consciousness is Universal Mind. Spiritual people call this power God; some scientists call it energy, and others cannot define it at all, although they have a feeling it exists. We are a part of this Great Intelligence. We have an incomprehensible relationship to it. It is within us, around us, and penetrates every living object. Religious Science teaches that God, the Universal Spirit, operates through a Universal Mind, which receives our thoughts and acts upon them, even communicates messages to us, through *intuition.*

The good news is that we don't have to wait for those messages to come to us; we can learn to tap into Universal Mind for all the answers we seek. As society's consciousness expands, more and more people will be benefiting from the effects of following their intuition. This capability has been lying dormant, waiting to be awakened. It is through intuition that we learn to disperse those erroneous influences which cause us to believe we are other than what we truly are. In the first stage of Self-realization it is necessary to have the intuitive power to discern ourselves as a pure conscious Being. When you learn how to access this power, it can change your life for the better, as it has changed mine.

Intuition is an inner power so deep, we have barely touched the surface of it in our human understanding—perhaps this is why so many students have found the subject fascinating. It manifests in several different ways. We shall focus on the following ways: clairsentience, clairvoyance, clairaudience, telepathy and psychometry.

CLAIRSENTIENCE

This word is derived from the French. *Clair* means clear, and *sentience* means sensing or feeling. Therefore, clairsentience means "clear feeling," or "clear sensing." This is what I experienced the night of Ken's marriage proposal. It can also be experienced as a sense of smell, taste, or a feeling, such as a tingling sensation or a cold chill. For example, you might smell flowers when there are no flowers around, and then later find yourself attending a funeral where the smell of flowers is the same as experienced beforehand.

Or, with the sense of taste, you might taste peppermint for no apparent reason, then later eat something that does not agree with you, and you end up drinking peppermint tea to soothe your stomach ache. In each of these examples, clairsentience served to warn you of a coming event.

Let's think about tingling or chills: When something happens that rings of a higher vibration, it causes a tingling or chill to the physical body. Some people call this "getting the goose bumps." This physical trigger alerts you to the fact that something special is happening. I often experience this sensation when I am predicting the future, and the tingling confirms my accuracy.

Other examples of clairsentience include hunches that turn out to be accurate:

…while in a public place, you suddenly feel the urge to turn your head and find   someone staring at you;

...when visiting a city for the first time, you have the feeling that you have been there before (deja vu);

...when you sense that a close friend or relative is in danger, you find out later that your feeling was correct.

CLAIRVOYANCE

Clairvoyance means "clear sight." It is seeing with the extended senses. This does not mean the ordinary physical senses, but rather the superphysical sense perceptions. For every one of the five senses, we have an extended sense that operates on a higher level of vibration than our physical realm. For instance, in metaphysical literature (metaphysical meaning beyond the physical, dealing with First Cause and Nature of Being), you will read about the "third eye." This refers to the *brow chakra,* located in the middle of the forehead. In Eastern studies the chakras are an intricate set of links or wheels of energy. These energy centers can be developed to allow superphysical perceptions to be brought through the subconscious to the waking mind. Once the brow chakra or energy center is awakened, you will begin to get clairvoyant flashes. For example, shortly after you get a flash of Aunt Blanche's face, you receive a letter from her. Many of my students experience clairvoyance, but, baffled by the event, dismiss it as their imagination.

Here is an exercise I have given to students in helping to develop clairvoyance. You will be predicting future events. Try this at the same time every day for thirty days. Sit down in an area where you won't be disturbed for five minutes. Take paper and pen and write down what you think could happen during the day. This could be an item of personal, local, national or international interest. Merely write down whatever comes to mind. All you need is a phrase or sentence; no need to elaborate unless you want to. Don't question or change what you write, even if it does not make sense to you. Clairvoyance is not always logical. At the end of the day check what you have written against the daily news.

A final word on this exercise: You may want to keep what you have written down for a few days. A prediction recorded on Monday could occur on Wednesday, Thursday, or even later. So, always give yourself a few days to see if your prediction will manifest. Time in metaphysics is not the same as time in the physical.

CLAIRAUDIENCE

Clairaudience means "clear hearing." During the beginning sessions of development classes, students hear sounds with the inner ear, such as someone calling their name. Then, when they look around, no one is visibly present. This can be an attempt of their spirit guide to help them experience the extended sense of hearing. Most often, this happens when a recently deceased loved one tries to ease the grief of a relative or close friend.

Educators have done research on how people process information. There is a correlation between how individuals process information and how intuition may manifest. This processing utilizes four means:

Visual - 70% of those tested *saw* the information (clairvoyance);

Auditory - 5% *heard* the information (clairaudience);

Kinetic - 24% *felt* a flow of energy (clairsentience);

Olfactory - 1% experienced through the sense of *smell* (clairsentience).

Students in development classes may think they are not getting results when they do not "see" anything in a clairvoyant or meditation exercise. So I ask them to think about what they may have heard or sensed, since each one processes development exercises in a different way. Then they often realize that they had a clairaudient or clairsentient experience.

TELEPATHY

This term is sometimes called *mental telepathy*. It refers to communication between one mind with another by some extraordinary means. The stronger the love between two people—for example, the bond between mother and child—the greater their ability to communicate through telepathy.

When I moved away from home to take a job, I often sent messages via telepathy instead of long-distance telephone calls. I would sit quietly and concentrate on visualizing my mother. As soon as I had a clear image of her in my mind, I would talk to her as if she were in the room with me. "Mom," I would tell her, "I am coming home this weekend. Look for me at eight o'clock on Friday night." Sure enough, she would be waiting for me when I arrived. I would ask her if she got the message, and she would confirm that she had.

Have you ever reached for the telephone, planning to call a friend or relative, and at that moment your telephone rings and it is that person calling you? If this has happened more than once, it is not coincidental; it was a manifestation of telepathy. You can develop telepathy by trying to guess who is on the other end of the line when your telephone rings.

PSYCHOMETRY

Psycho means "soul" and the suffix *metry* means "measure." Psychometry, then, is measuring the soul or reading personal vibrations by attuning to an object worn by a person. We are broadcasting messages about ourselves every minute through electromagnetic vibrations, although we may not be aware of it. Whenever the subject of psychometry comes up, my thoughts go back to the day I met Reverend Hill.

Dora sent me to the reverend, a talented clairvoyant, when she knew I was ready for a "reading." It did not turn out to be what I expected. The plump, white-haired woman proudly displayed her certificate as minister of Spiritual Science. She had earned her degree after many years of intense study. Reverend Hill asked to hold my watch or ring—something I wore often—during the reading. I handed her my watch.

She explained that she performed intuitive readings through psychometry. By holding an article I had been wearing she could become attuned to my vibrations. I was like a radio station, she said, and she was the listener, tuning in to the

8

electromagnetic vibrations that were being broadcast from my conscious and subconscious mind.

Reverend Hill closed her eyes, then said, "This was given to you by someone who loves you."

That was correct; the watch was from my mother. A little skeptical, I reasoned that this woman was a good guesser. The rest of the reading, however, canceled any doubt I had about Reverend Hill.

She closed her eyes and stiffened. "Oh, my dear, you have had thoughts of suicide!"

I was alarmed. How could she know about *that*?

Noticing my uneasiness, she said, "It's OK, we don't have to go into it if you don't want to."

I shook my head no and breathed a long sigh. It wasn't something I wanted to dwell on. (This will be more clear in the section on prayer.)

"Let me explain something about suicide. Each one of us comes into embodiment for a particular purpose while on the earth plane. When someone commits suicide, it interferes with the Divine Will for that individual.

"A great price is paid for the mistake of trying to escape life's problems and lessons. In actuality, there is no escape, because when you pass over to the other side of life, whatever state of mind you possessed goes over with you. Without the physical body that acts as a shield, everything is amplified. Your thoughts and emotions are amplified. So, if you are in mental pain at the time of suicide, it becomes more painful when you reach the spirit side of life. Your past is reviewed, and nothing can be hidden. This review is for your soul to understand what has been done with your life through your actions.

"All forms of matter come to an end under the Law of Cycles. Death of the physical takes place from two causes," the Reverend went on. "One, you have reached the end of your physical cycle, and you are given an opportunity for something new, a rebirth. Secondly, you have misused energy or taken deliberate action against life, as in suicide.

"Many people don't understand that misusing energy, such as abusing the body through harmful drugs, is a form of suicide. And few understand that suicide is a form of murder. Murdering yourself carries as heavy a burden as killing another person. When you take away a life, the deed has to be reckoned with. Even if you escape punishment on the physical plane, you will face it on the spiritual plane of existence.

"I see that you received an enormous amount of spiritual help during that period of trial when you considered taking your own life. You were helped because you needed more time to realize your purpose in life."

Reverend Hill took a deep breath and was silent for a few minutes. Then, suddenly, she yelled, "You can do this!"

I sat up in my chair, not knowing what she meant.

"Yes," she affirmed, "You have the gift of psychometry! You can sense things about people and be very accurate. You will find psychometry easy to use as a tool for your intuition.

She urged me to try it. "You are interested in developing your intuitive skills, and that is what brought you here."

"Yes, but—" I protested.

"My dear, it's time for you to go to work on developing your natural gifts and talents. An opportunity will present itself very soon."

And so it was settled.

My reading turned into a lesson on psychometry.

Just before the end of the lesson she told me, "The experience of intuitive power is unique for each person. It can also manifest through the creative arts such as painting or writing, through dreams, or in meditation through the still voice which can stabilize us through life's struggles."

Why don't more people tap into their intuition to guide them, since we all have this latent power? Many individuals do not know how to begin to develop their skills. Reverend Hill gave me a technique to use to develop my intuition, and now I am passing it on to you.

CENTERING: ATTUNING TO YOUR INNER POWER

Tapping into your inner power depends on the use of four basic procedures: (1) balancing energy, (2) relaxing your body, (3) making your mind passive, and (4) focusing your attention.

(1) **Balancing energy.** Alignment of energy removes uneven energy patterns in the body. Our bodies have an electromagnetic field of energy. The left side of the physical body has a negative charge; the right side has a positive charge. We can create a strong magnetic field of energy by putting these two charges together. It is the same effect as putting together the opposite ends of a magnet. This is accomplished by putting your hands together, in a prayer position, fingertips pointing straight up, with the thumbs and fingers aligned exactly opposite. Hold this position for five minutes.

Each side of your body has a unique rhythm. Take a moment to feel the rhythm of the left side of the body, which receives energy. Next, take a moment to feel the rhythm of the right side of your body, which gives energy. Notice how the flow of energy feels. Hold the hands apart, about one-fourth of an inch to see if the energy feels balanced, or unbalanced. If it is unbalanced, one of the hands will vibrate more than the other.

Now put the hands together again. Make sure that your legs are uncrossed all the while you are doing this. Allow the energies of each hand to flow into a smooth rhythm for another three minutes. This brings your body into balance and harmony so that you are ready for the next procedure.

(2) **Relaxing your body.** Find a quiet place where you can be alone. Settle into a comfortable chair. Then picture a golden-white ray from the sun coming down over your head, shoulders, mid-section, and down through your feet. Think: *I am still.*

(3) **Making your mind passive.** Close your eyes and take three deep breaths. In your mind's eye, put all stray thoughts into a large purple balloon. See the balloon carrying them away.

11

(4) **Focusing your attention.** Focus your attention on a spot in the center of your forehead, where mental images are received and created. Envision a blank television screen. Ask yourself a question to which you would like to receive an answer. Make a mental or written note of any impressions you may see, hear or feel.

When you are trying to guess who is calling on the phone, see a blank TV screen and wait for the picture of the person to appear. (You may even hear a voice that tells you the name of the person.) If you are trying to attune to history or events by holding a physical object, picture the owner of the object. Then look for what manifests on the blank screen.

Do not try to force impressions. Let them happen naturally. Your first impression is usually the correct one. Write it down right away before your conscious mind tries to talk you out of it. Remember that this technique involves working with your subconscious mind, which is not limited by time or space. You can receive a thought from someone two thousand miles away just as easily as from someone two blocks away. If no impression is received, try again at a later time.

A cautionary measure: Always analyze your impressions to make certain that your worries or wishful thinking are not what is coming through. As we proceed further, you will understand the difference between worry thoughts and true guidance.

Interestingly, a few weeks after my visit with Reverend Hill, the opportunity came to use my newfound skills, as she had predicted. I was with some friends at Sam's, a popular hangout for college students and locals in Elmira, New York. Its pizza and jukebox attracted a lot of young people on weekends. On this particular night, I was sitting with my friends when a young man asked me to dance. Something about him was attractive, so I danced with him. Afterwards, he introduced himself as Earl, and joined me and my friends at our table. We had such a good time, he asked me for a date. My instinctive response was yes.

The following Saturday night, Earl took me to a fabulous Italian restaurant. While we were waiting for our dinner, he asked, "Do you know why I asked you to dance at Sam's?"

"No... why?"

"I saw this white light above your head, and it drew me to you."

I sat there astonished. No one had ever told me that before, although it was to happen a few more times when I encountered individuals with special powers of perception. Only after I became more knowledgeable, did I understand that he saw the light of the oversoul. (An explanation of the oversoul is found in Treasure Number Four.)

"Anyway," Earl said, "I feel as if I am supposed to learn something from you."

Our conversation turned to intuition and some of the things I had learned. He was fascinated when I told him about psychometry. At that moment I had a very strong urge to put psychometry to the test.

"Hand me your watch," I said.

Earl looked so surprised, I almost chickened out. But I recalled Reverend Hill's words, "When people react that way, just follow your feelings." She also had told me that I would be led to the right person with whom to share intuitive impressions and added, "The more you share, the more you receive."

Earl handed me his watch, as he joked, "I don't know why I should trust you with this."

As soon as I held his watch in my hand, I followed Reverend Hill's instructions. I closed my eyes and tried to attune to Earl through his watch. Quite suddenly, I saw a picture of a woman who wore her hair pulled back in a bun. I described what I was seeing.

Earl's eyes widened. "Do you know *who* you are seeing?"

"No," I answered. "Tell me."

"My mother. She passed away a few years ago. And she gave me that watch."

At that point I was as stunned as he was. Here was a confirmation that I had accurately picked up Earl's vibrations.

Life went on that way. As soon as I accepted that I had a special power within me, and committed myself to nurturing it, certain people appeared in my life to help me develop and grow. I learned that everything that happens to us has a purpose, a reason. There are no coincidences; the Creator has a purpose for everything that comes into our life.

We all share a universal purpose, to master life on the earth plane. Achieving mastery enables us to rise to any challenge. The only way to conquer the physical or earth plane is through the spirit. To know the spirit, you need to know God.

If you have been called to read this book, then you have already set your foot on the road to mastery. As you develop your intuition, you come to a point where you will no longer rely on a teacher outside yourself. Instead, you will begin to listen to the still voice within and know the meaning of "Be still and know that I am God."

SUMMARY

Intuitive skills will be needed in the twenty-first century. Intuition is our guiding light, the key that unlocks the door to spiritual mastery. Our awareness increases through this creative power, enabling us to perceive the higher dimensions of life, where needs are met and peace is found.

Intuitive power can be developed with practice. It can manifest through clairsentience, clairvoyance, clairaudience, telepathy, or psychometry. You can attune to this inner power through *centering*—a technique of balancing energy, relaxing, making the mind passive, and focusing your attention.

With practice and experience, you will know how to rely on your intuition. You will understand that the Universe speaks to you through people, events, and things that seem like coincidences. In reality, they are part of God's plan for your development to lead you to a higher state of consciousness and awareness.

We enter a state of higher awareness when we can attune to the inner voice within. One of the ways in which we can sharpen our awareness is through the act of decision-making.

Would you like to find easier ways to make decisions? Helpful knowledge awaits you in the next treasure.

TREASURE NUMBER TWO: *MAKING DECISIONS EASIER*

I will but ask clear light from heaven to show
How step by step my pilgrimage should go.

--Anon.

Are there times when you have difficulty making a decision? Are you so worried about making the right choice that your mind goes blank? Or do you sometimes reach a decision, then a gut feeling pulls you back? The confusion can be paralyzing.

The secret to making good decisions is gathering accurate information, then using your intuition. Blend worldly knowledge with inner knowledge. Use the creative part of your brain to select possible choices from the data you have gathered. After you have collected the best information, you are ready to consult your inner voice.

Often people learn to follow their intuition because they recall mistakes made when they ignored those "gut feelings." These gut feelings come from the solar plexus, which is comprised of a network of nerves located at the upper part of the abdomen, behind the stomach and in front of the aorta. This is such a powerful nerve center, that a blow to this area can cause real physical damage to the body. The solar plexus is one of the major chakras (energy centers) important to Chinese acupuncture and Eastern forms of meditation. The subconscious mind and the solar plexus are working together when we get a sensation in the pit of the stomach.

Here is a decision-making exercise to test your gut feelings:

PENDULUM EXERCISE

You will need a pendulum, an object suspended from a chain that is able to swing back and forth by the action of gravity and energy. You can use a crystal or any pendant on a chain, or make your own pendulum. With sewing thread, make the thread eight inches long after doubling it. Then poke it through a large button with two eyes. Tie a knot at the end of the thread. The pendulum works best when the button hangs from the center of the thread, and its weight is evenly distributed.

1. Find a quiet place where you can be alone and comfortable. Relax. Let go of all concerns. Breathe deeply and gently, in through the nose and out through the mouth three times. Picture a white bubble of light encompassing your whole body. You are in the center of this bubble of light.

2. Sit at a table with pen or pencil and a blank sheet of writing paper. Draw a circle with a line running North and South. Then draw a line running East and West. One line will represent yes; the other line will represent no. It will look like A or B in the diagram below, depending on the direction you get in Step 3.

3. Hold the thread or chain of the pendulum slightly above the writing paper with your writing hand. Say, "Universal Mind, in which direction will you move when the answer is yes?" Note which direction the pendulum moves. Look for a definite North and South direction, or East and West. (If the pendulum goes around in a circle, you are not concentrating enough). Label the definite direction as yes, and the opposite direction as no.

4. Select a decision you want to make. Ask a question that can be answered with a simple yes or no. Phrase your question carefully. For example: "Is it for my highest good to accept the new job being offered to me?" Let your mind go blank after you ask the question in order for the subconscious to respond and allow the pendulum to swing in the correct direction. Sometimes the pendulum will swing around in a circle, which means, "I don't know," or lack of concentration. Sooner or later, the pendulum will indicate a more definite answer through patience. If you are doing this when you are tired, the pendulum may go around in a circle or just stop. In such cases, try again when rested.

Exactly why the pendulum works is a mystery, except that the subconscious mind can work through the extended senses, beyond the realm of the five senses. The subconscious mind and the solar plexus hold more power than is presently understood, and the pendulum can serve as a channel for this power.

PENDULUM DIAGRAM

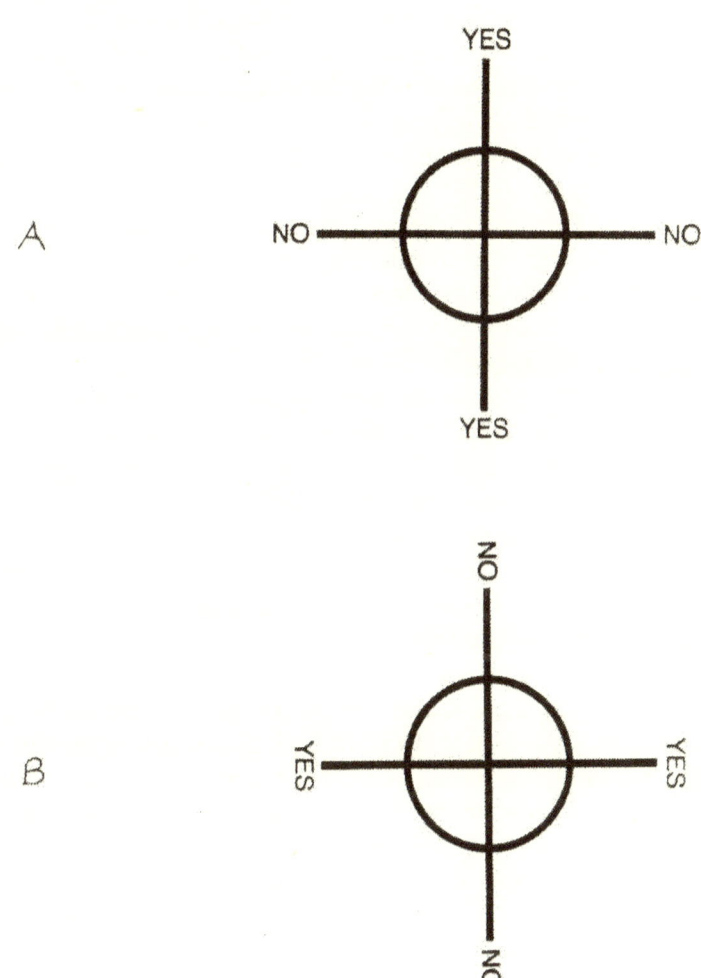

Because each person's magnetic field is different, the pendulum swing response may be the opposite for one person than it is for another person. You can determine your personal response by asking Universal Mind, or by asking a question to which you know the answer, such as, "Is my name………." And label the yes or no direction accordingly.

THE POWER OF DREAMS TO MAKE A DECISION

The fascination and mystery of dreams goes back to ancient times. The Egyptians and other ancient civilizations had seers who were devoted to the task of interpreting dreams. The pharaohs relied heavily on their seers for guidance and making decisions.

The Greeks had dream centers called Asklepian temples where dreaming was directed by trained individuals. The Greeks had learned to use dreams for healing purposes. This is where the practice of "Dream Incubation" began, which is used by psychologists today.

The Bible contains many passages where men were guided by dreams. One example is the passage where an angel appeared to Joseph and instructed him to take Jesus to Egypt to save His life from the threat of King Herod. (Matthew: 2:13)

Robert Louis Stevenson and Thomas Edison used dreams as pathways to answers. Every night we, too, have the opportunity to receive guidance from Universal Mind. The more we understand and use this guidance, the more help we receive. Dreams give birth to an inner autobiography that can increase intuition, self-awareness, and offer guidance in decision-making.

Research shows that we have from five to seven dreams a night, but rarely do we remember their content. We have to let our subconscious mind know that we are ready to work with it. With practice we can cue the subconscious mind to help us receive needed answers through dreams.

There is no limit to the functioning of your subconscious mind when given direction before entering the sleep state. Many scientists who could not solve a problem in the waking state have "gone to sleep on it" and then had the answer revealed in a dream.

DREAM INCUBATION

(1) Prior to bedtime, select a specific question to pose to your subconscious during sleep. Be definite and write it down. The act of setting it to paper signals to your subconscious that this is important to you. Read the question out loud and with feeling. Then put the paper under your pillow.

(2) Say to yourself, "I will remember my dream. I ask Universal Mind to reveal the answer I need in such a way that I can remember and understand it."

(3) Keep paper and pencil at your bedside and write down any strong feelings you have upon awakening. Immediately record everything you remember from the dream. Also, be alert for clues throughout the day; something or someone may remind you of the dream, or you may read a word or phrase in an article that will trigger remembrance.

(4) When you first awaken, remain in the same position you were in when you woke up. Many of my students have found that it helps to remember the dream when they do this.

In the event you do not have dream recall, upon awakening, ask yourself, "What is my answer?" Listen for an inner reply, then write it down.

If you do not receive an answer, repeat steps one and two on the following night. If this is the first time you have attempted to work with your subconscious, be aware that some students have needed to repeat the procedure for at least three nights before receiving an answer.

A student named Helen programmed her subconscious mind for dreaming when she had to decide whether or not to have an operation. On the third night her brother appeared in a dream and told her to have the operation, that it would be successful. She knew upon awakening that having the operation was the answer, and it did provide the results she sought.

Often a loved one or family member gives guidance in a dream. Other students report having an angel deliver a message in a dream.

Keeping a journal of your dreams can help you get in touch with the message of each dream. Many books on the market can help you analyze your dreams and their symbols. One book I found most helpful to students in dream workshops is *Dreams Your Magic Mirror* by Elsie Sechrist.

DREAM JOURNAL OUTLINE

A dream is often like a stage play with a setting, background, characters or players, props, action, dialog, mood and theme. After thinking about your dream, ask yourself the following questions:

What was the setting of the dream? Where did it take place?

Who were the players such as people, animals, etc.?

What were the props—objects that were noticeably part of the theme?

What action took place?

What colors, shapes, sizes were noticeable?

What was said in the dream and who said it?

What was the time of day? Was it morning, evening, past or present?

What appeared right, left, behind or straight ahead? (Usually the right represents the future and the left represents the past.)

What was the mood or emotion expressed? Did you feel happy, sad, angry, etc.?

Draw a diagram to help describe the dream. What were the phrases or symbols that stood out?

Our dreams contain symbols because this is the way that the subconscious mind records our experiences, thoughts and impressions. Symbols are codes that often have a deeper meaning that what appears on the surface. Because of this, a symbol can have more than one meaning and can be both positive and negative due to the duality of our earthly existence.

For example, many people dream of snakes. To people in the Western world, it can mean fear or danger. To people in the Middle East, it can mean good luck or wisdom because they view snakes in a positive light, while the Western Hemisphere tends to view them in a negative light. It all depends on your accustomed way of thinking.

Other points to ponder in working with guidance dreams:
    *Messages in dreams take place in the hypnogogic state of consciousness that occurs between waking and sleeping. Sometimes it helps to retire one half-hour earlier than usual. Or you might try sleeping 30 minutes later in the morning to allow more time for this state of heightened awareness.
    *If you cannot interpret the messages in your dream, ask for clarification in another dream, in quiet time or meditation. Be on the lookout for confirmation or clues regarding messages throughout the next day. Something you see, hear or read may trigger recall.
    *Contact your local bookstore or gem store to see if they have a Herkimer diamond, which is an inexpensive quartz crystal. This has been known to spur dream remembrance when placed around the pillow. You may also want to ask if they have a dream catcher, a Native American ornament that can be hung in the bedroom to enhance your dream activity.
    *As you improve in dream analysis, you may receive telepathic or clairaudient messages. These are intuitive skills that develop in the dream state when you meditate during the day. So it would be advantageous for you to practice meditation to accelerate your dreaming results, too.

VISUALIZATION TECHNIQUE
    Here is a visualization I suggested to James, a client, who had to make a decision on whether or not to get a divorce. James recorded the words on tape, then closed his eyes and listened to the following:
    Situate yourself in a quiet place. This will work best if you are sitting in a chair with your spine straight and your

feet flat on the floor. As soon as you feel comfortable, think about the decision you have to make. Then say to yourself: "I am relaxed. My neck and shoulders are heavy and warm. My arms are heavy and warm. My legs are heavy and warm. My abdomen is warm. My forehead is cool."

Picture yourself standing at the foot of a mountain. The sun is shining in all its glory, and you feel it shower its rays of golden-white light upon you, from head to toe. You start slowly to ascend the mountain. There is a certain joy in nature as you notice a bird singing. A gentle wind stirs the trees. As you climb higher on the path, you smell the scent of the pine trees, which is both relaxing and invigorating. Soon you reach the top of the mountain. You notice a person sitting on a log bench. This person beckons you to come and sit down. You sense this is a person of great wisdom. So you go over and sit down on the log bench. You sit together and enjoy a feeling like that of being with a close friend. The importance of making a decision comes into your mind. You feel open enough with this person to ask what your decision should be, in order to bring the highest good into your life. You know this person knows the answer. You wait a few moments and then the answer becomes clear. This person has the ability to speak to you so that you may hear the answer, or you may be shown a symbol, or you may sense or feel the answer. After your question gets answered, you thank this person of great wisdom. You are invited to return to this place on the mountain whenever you have the need to make a decision. You bid each other goodbye. Then you start to make your way down the mountain. As you descend the mountain, you feel the brightness of the sun on your body. You are filled with joy. As you continue to descend the mountain you notice a pleasant floral scent and you feel very refreshed. You feel wonderful, knowing that you can return to this peaceful setting whenever you need to receive clear answers. The person of great wisdom will be there whenever you want. Next, you bring your attention back to the place you have chosen for this quiet visualization, and,

when you feel ready, open your eyes. Recall the answer from the wise person, and jot it down on paper.

I always find it fascinating to learn how each client or student experiences the wise person. James was delighted with the results of this visualization. He told me that he saw the wise person as an old man who was tall, had a white beard, clear eyes and wore a brown robe. He told James to have faith; the problems with his wife would be remedied. The wise man said to pray and meditate for deeper knowledge of what action to take. He went on to say that if James would make some necessary changes, the marriage would greatly improve and no divorce would be needed. James followed the advice and became very happy in the renewed relationship.

LAST BUT NOT LEAST

When in urgent need of an answer or inspiration, ask yourself what your spiritual role model would do about this situation. For instance, when I am faced with a dilemma while teaching, I will silently say, "What would Jesus do?" This provides me access to my higher mind, which in turn produces a creative idea. It gives me a sense of fulfillment to get results this way.

Another way to do this is to close your eyes and visualize yourself walking along a beach. As you walk along the beach, you can feel the warm sun on your back. There is a cool breeze stirring, and you feel it brush across your face. Away in the distance you can see the figure of a person walking toward you. You sense it is someone you know but can't see them clearly. As the person comes nearer and nearer to you, you begin to recognize who it is. Finally it is more clear. You see it is Jesus, and you begin to walk faster. Then you are running toward Him. As you meet Him, you both embrace. You ask Jesus how to make a decision on something that is on your mind. Jesus tells you that He is going to write you a letter. With pen and paper write down what you think Jesus would write to you to help you in your decision. Take your time and let your imagination flow.

You may be surprised at what results you get from this technique.

SUMMARY

Intuition is a treasure that can guide you in making important decisions in your life through the pendulum, the power of dreams, or visualization techniques, such as the mountain visualization. As you do the exercises in this treasure, you can evoke intuitive guidance and receive its rewards.

The more you learn to trust and follow the guidance of your inner voice, the more frequently you will receive helpful inspirations and contact with the Presence of God, which brings its own peace. You can learn how to build on this through prayer, meditation and contemplation in the following additional treasures.

SECTION TWO: CREATING INNER PEACE

TREASURE NUMBER THREE: *P R A Y E R*

"The kingdom of God is within you."

--Luke, 17:21

Are you happy?

In order to answer this question, let's define happiness. Happiness is an enduring feeling of contentment, joy, hope and peace. We all know people who have found happiness. How did they get it? The happy ones have discovered how to flow *with* the universe, rather than *against* the universe. They have learned how to use events as stepping stones, instead of resisting or blocking their highest good as it flows from the universe.

Most of us will agree that people want to be happy. But according to Dennis Wholey, author of *Are You Happy*, research shows that only about twenty percent of Americans are happy. What is the reason for such a small percentage of happy people?

The average person's happiness is determined by favorable circumstances. They crave a peaceful life, with a loving family and friends and congenial co-workers. But as soon as a problem comes along, they are unhappy.

Is it possible to stay peaceful and firm when something rocks our boat? We know the answer is yes, for we have all met people whose existence seems steady, balanced, secure. No matter what happens to them, they enjoy a strength and a clarity that we respect, admire, and wish we had too.

How can we stay centered in spite of the change, uncertainty and turmoil we must face simply because we are alive and interacting with a troubled society?

An awakening is needed within ourselves and society. Many individuals believe that the prime purpose in life is physical gratification, and the media support that view. As a result, our body gets a lot of attention. A thousand television commercials tell us what to do for our hips, thighs, teeth, hair, complexion and armpits. Magazine advertisements tell us that we must look young and beautiful in order to be happy in life.

Yet somewhere in time we realize that physical beauty fades. It is only *spiritual* beauty that is everlasting—you don't have to buy it; you only have to learn how to draw it forth.

Spiritual beauty has been a quest for individuals who know that treasures are found in the enriching interior life, which can take you to intriguing places without your leaving home.

WHAT IS THE SOURCE OF CONTENTMENT?

Modern society is on a collision course on how to please the body, but little effort is made to satisfy the soul. As time progresses, the soul cries out for attention. And if it takes a tragedy to get attention, something tragic will occur. I know people who have experienced accidents, or health problems as wake-up calls to get in touch with God, the true source of contentment. Genuine happiness depends on our relationship with this Higher Power.

Why put yourself through unnecessary struggles? Why not learn how to balance your attention to include both the soul and the body? We need to exercise our spiritual nature, as well as our physical self, in order to be whole. We know how to improve physical fitness, but what about spiritual fitness? If we do not take time to go within, we go without the best that the universe has to offer. Happiness comes from experiencing our true spiritual nature and knowing how to express it through our life purpose. Problems then become opportunities or lessons leading to spiritual growth.

When we have a relationship with God, we experience one great spiritual truth: **We are divine spiritual beings temporarily relating to the human experience of earth**. Don't take this lightly. You are much more than you are expressing in your physical experience. This will become more clear as we proceed.

As a young girl, I was taught that prayer is the lifting of our voices, minds and hearts to God. Another way to look at prayer would be: Prayer is getting centered, in touch with that individualized portion of God that is anchored in our hearts. How do we get in touch with God? By acknowledging that the

Infinite is already *within us*, not outside us in the clouds somewhere. Our soul nature is God-individualized. Once we accept that God is already a part of us, we can experience the presence of God through our awareness of this special relationship.

How do we develop the awareness of our relationship with God? We begin with prayer.

We have three tools that we can use to increase our awareness between the soul and God: prayer, meditation, and contemplation. These tools help to create a still, inner environment where we can lay the groundwork for a life of peace.

In vocal *prayer,* we lift our voices to God. In *meditation,* we lift our minds to God. In *contemplation,* we lift our hearts to God by expressing our innermost feelings, our most heartfelt prayer. God created us with the gift of free will. Because of this, we have to make the first step toward God, and prayer is the perfect place to start.

WHAT IS PRAYER?

Prayer is opening the line of communication to God. How could you call someone on the telephone if you did not pick up the phone and dial to make the connection? Think of prayer as a phone call to the Chief Executive Officer in Central Office.

One of the first points I make to students is that we should never hesitate to call on God, whatever the need, whatever the hour. It is surprising how many individuals get the notion that God is too busy to hear their prayers...or that God will pass them over in favor of someone in greater need...or that God will not consider them worthy of having their prayers answered—all negative concepts picked up somewhere.

THE DYNAMIC POWER OF PRAYER

One day I got caught in a downhill slump. I prayed, telling God that I was having a hard time and asked for something to happen to lift my spirits. A little while later, the telephone rang—a long-distance call from a former student. She said just the right words that helped me that day. Where did she get the knowledge to call me and to use the words I needed? God was working through her to answer prayer. The Chief Executive Officer got her attention and inspired her to call me.

I have experienced complex as well as simple answers to prayer. I was told by my doctor that I needed to have an ovarian cyst removed and the ovary itself. Feeling panicky and not wanting the surgery, I told the doctor to wait a few months. He warned me that the cyst could become more threatening, and he scheduled the operation to take place in two months. I decided to work with prayer and mental healing on my medical condition.

Through prayer, I reinforced my connection to God, who is all-powerful and perfect. The statement, "With God all things are possible," kept going through my mind. By calling on God and the healing angels, I was opening a channel for the release of cosmic rays to heal and bless my body.

Next, I looked in my Spiritual Science lessons to find the metaphysical cause for cysts. My literature described cysts as growths from negative thought patterns, caused by repeated dwelling on pain and hurts. As soon as I realized that I needed to forgive someone who had hurt me, I changed my negative thought patterns. I had learned that our enemies can be our greatest teachers, so I began to see this enemy in a positive light. I saw this problem as training to help me acquire peace.

Forgiveness is necessary for inner peace and healing. Therefore, I accepted that I was responsible for my health. I could not change what people did, but I could change how I reacted. Every outward manifestation is a result of some inner thought or consciousness. I had the power to bring something negative into my life; now I realized I had the power to transform it into something positive.

After praying to God and forgiving the one who had hurt me, I concentrated on the mental healing. Every day I mentally pictured the ovary as healed and perfect, and the cyst entirely gone. I had learned that repetitive thought patterns create life experiences; by repeating positive thought patterns, along with prayer, I had faith that I could change this experience from negative to positive.

A week before the operation was scheduled, I insisted that my doctor examine me. He was astounded that the cyst was gone, and he canceled the surgery. Halleluia!

A MIRACULOUS HEALING THROUGH PRAYER

Prayer saved my life. When I was nineteen years old, I left home for the first time and moved to California. I had been raised in a small city in New York state, where life was happy and easygoing; therefore, I was not prepared for some of the difficulties I came to encounter.

My job began as a nine-to-five setup, then evolved into working three different shifts every three days. The graveyard shift (from midnight to 8 a.m.) wrecked me. My sleep patterns were destroyed, and I began to hate my job. In addition, I was homesick. Soon I had the symptoms of hysteroneurosis, a uterine disorder, which left me exceedingly depressed. The excruciating pain led to thoughts of suicide. (This is the event perceived by Reverend Hill during that uncanny psychometry reading.)

My mother and I were communicating by letters and long-distance phone calls. Worried about my declining physical and mental health, she visited Mount Savior Monastery in Big Flats, New York, and spoke to a monk about my situation. She asked him to pray for me, and he assured her that the entire monastic community would put me in prayer. Meanwhile, I had no inkling of what had my mother had done.

A few days after her visit to Mount Savior, Mother Mary appeared to me in a dream. She looked absolutely beautiful in a rose-gold gown with a green cape, and a magnificent white light shining around her. Her presence was so real that I could sense her peace. While bathing in her soothing, calming radiance, I could actually feel a healing taking place in my body.

She showed me scenes of the future, and one in particular remains locked in my memory: I was traveling home, to the street where my family lived. As soon as I realized that Mother Mary was telling me to return home, the scene faded...although

I could still see her at the foot of my bed. Her smile was so uplifting, I began to smile myself. She told me that everything would be all right. I knew that I was no longer alone; she would help me.

I was awakening. The more conscious I became, the more her form began to fade, very slowly, until all that remained was a pure white light at the foot of the bed.

The light stayed with me for a while, pleasant and comforting, then evaporated. I felt so joyful with this newfound peace. After several days, during which the feeling stayed with me, I wrote this poem:

THE VISITATION

It happened on one morning rare
When God sent the Mother to answer prayer.
There was no doubt that I was heard,
As She spoke to me in gentle word.

My heart cried out: Why am I a mess?
She said, "Do not fret, I came to bless.
The sufferings you have endured,
Are over now….You are cured.

"You searched for purpose, your cause to roam.
Do not be tempted to stay—go home.
Many truths yet you need to know.
Allow me to show you where to go.

"Happiness will not be as you think it ought.
But victories will be won as the soul has sought.
Few know their reason for being on earth.
But you will, later, in joy and mirth.

"Go forth and know that I am with you,
Just as I promised to help those who
Take time to pray to The Lord and me,
And you will receive help through eternity."

A transformation had taken place. I had been healed both physically and mentally. I felt so good, I was tempted to try to work things out in California. I did not want people to say that I could not make it on the West Coast. But Mother Mary brought the message back to my mind to go home, and told me not to worry about such things. Only ego causes us to worry about what other people think of us. Something more was involved in the need for me to return home—my spiritual growth. As soon as I understood this, I felt a renewed purpose in living.

Many prayers and calls were made those days in California, and they had been answered in a miraculous way. The act of praying deeply, with faith, brings exceptional life-altering experiences. It is important to know that we are not alone in life. Friends, family, associates, or spiritual beings (such as angels, Buddha, Jesus, Mother Mary) are always ready to help, and they are only a prayer away.

PRAYER STEPS THAT NEVER FAIL

Some individuals feel skeptical about the power of prayer because their prayers are not answered. Usually these people do not pray enough or do not know how to pray effectively. The following are proven steps to bring you successful results.

(1) *Recognize that faith is needed.* No prayer or healing can be successful without faith. This means praying without doubt or fear. We need only to look in the newspaper to find evidence of prayerful results: Jeremiah Bell, a Bradenton, Florida teenager, slipped into a coma after drinking a concoction of poisonous mushrooms in March, 1997. The prognosis was not good. He almost died because his liver was destroyed from the toxic effect of the mushrooms. While Bell lay comatose in the hospital for nine days, his family prayed for his recovery with unfaltering faith. After an emergency transplant, Bell awoke from the coma with no brain damage and renewed hope for his future. Through faith and prayer, Bell was miraculously healed, and his

family was enabled to get through the ordeal. The whole family became stronger as a result of the experience.

(2) *Clear yourself of negative patterns* that prevent positive results. Have you heard about the impatient man who planted a seed but kept digging it up to see if it had sprouted yet? When we are anxious or doubtful, we are like that impatient man who prevented the seed from growing into what it was intended to be. Visualize your prayer as a seed that you are putting in God's hands. Then release doubt, anxiety, worry or any negative emotions from your mind. Patience will bring the desired outcome.

(3) *Be forgiving.* Are you harboring a grudge? If you are, it will stand in the way of positive results by blocking your positive flow of energy. Learn to forgive any injustice "…lest any root or bitterness springing up cause trouble…" (Hebrews 12:15) Bitterness causes emotional damage. Paul made a point of getting rid of bitterness quickly in Ephesians 4:26, "Do not let the sun go down on your wrath."

(4) *Decide what you want, then visualize it as a reality.* There is power in focusing on a clear goal. At the time you utter it, see your prayer getting answered. While your logical mind may have a tendency to doubt that prayers will materialize, remind yourself that you will not accept thoughts which oppose your goal. As you believe in your heart, it will be done to you. What you think and feel, you bring into form.

(5) *Be persistent.* The Bible tells us to pray without ceasing. We have numerous opportunities to pray during the day: upon awakening, before meals, when some need arises, before a challenging task, before expressing anger, before traveling, or before going to sleep. The following quote is attributed to Calvin Coolidge, the 30th President of the United States:

"Nothing in the world can take the place of persistence. Talent will not; nothing is more common than unsuccessful men with talent. Genius will not; unrewarded genius is almost a proverb. Education alone will not; the world is full of educated derelicts. Persistence and determination alone are omnipotent! The slogan 'press on' has solved and always will solve the problems of the human race."

Many of the world's prayers have gone unanswered because people gave up too soon. You will be the squeaky wheel that gets the grease if you continue to press on.

(6) *Ask others to pray with you.* If there is power in prayer when one person prays, imagine the power when several people pray! The more people praying for a common purpose, the more dynamic the prayer. When you have an especially difficult problem, ask others who have your best interests at heart to help. Besides family, friends and associates, church prayer groups are willing to help. Sometimes the extra power of teamwork is the bolt of lightning needed to transform those tougher problems into miracles. And why do miracles happen? Miracles occur to give witness to God's awesome power of healing through faith. When we open our minds to unlimited possibilities, miracles are allowed to flow through the rhythm of the universe.

One evening I was demonstrating to a class how to form a healing circle by having twelve students join hands. A woman asked us to pray for her grandchild, who was in the hospital with a mysterious heart problem. We pictured him in the center of our circle and sent loving thoughts to him. We prayed that he would be restored to perfect health. The next week the grandmother returned to class and, filled with excitement, told us that the boy had been healed and sent home by puzzled doctors.

This dynamic power of prayer through teamwork also had been working when Mother Mary appeared in my dream. I had been praying, as were my mother and the monks.

(7) *Give thanks.* Most people remember to express gratitude *after* prayer is answered, but it is important to give thanks at the end of your prayer *before* the request is granted. By doing this you are acknowledging that your good already exists and is on its way to you. The special power in

thanksgiving is mentioned in the Bible: "He took the seven loaves and the fish, and *having given thanks* he broke them and gave them to the disciples, and the disciples gave them to the crowds." (Matthew 15:36)

This was the miracle of the multiplication of the loaves and fishes, or what is referred to as "precipitation." Seven loaves and one fish represent the seed that was multiplied a hundred-fold to feed a large crowd of people.

(8) *Pray for God's Will for miraculous solutions to problems.* On December 16, 1995, a television program, *Larry King Weekend*, focused on the subject of miracles. One of the guests was Dr. Larry Dossey, a former chief of staff at Medical City Dallas Hospital in Texas, and author of *Healing Words: The Power of Prayer and the Practice of Medicine* (Harper San Francisco, 1993). Dr. Dossey said that one-third of the medical schools have developed alternative medicine and the study of miracles. He went on to say that research shows that we do not need to pray for something specific. We can pray for God's Will or our highest good to bring miraculous results, because the Universe knows how to respond to needs which we do not know how to fill.

We can easily recognize that there are many methods and ways to pray. It does not have to be an enormous effort. It can be the most simple prayer. But if you want to insure effective results, here is a summary of the eight steps:

1) recognize that faith is needed;
2) clear yourself of negative patterns;
3) be forgiving;
4) decide what you want, then visualize it as a reality;
5) be persistent;
6) ask others to pray with you;
7) give thanks;

8) pray for God's Will for miraculous solutions to problems.

The significant point is that prayer works. When someone is praying for me, I can feel a peaceful energy in the crown chakra of the head. Prayer is a wonderful tool that we can utilize for almost any need. And it can bring us a treasure of peace, not found in any other way.

A FINAL THOUGHT FROM A WELL-KNOWN EXPERT ON PRAYER

A few years ago, I wrote to Mother Teresa of Calcutta asking for her permission to use one of her quotes in my writings. Along with her permission, she sent a prayer that said, "LOVE TO PRAY—feel often during the day the need for prayer and take trouble to pray. Prayer enlarges the heart until it is capable of containing God's gift of Himself."

And then, as an added bonus, Mother Teresa wrote me a personal message in her own words: **"Keep the joy of loving Jesus, and of being loved by Him, always in your heart and share that joy with all you meet. God bless you!"**

God is the source of love. What can you do when it seems that you live in a world without love? Go into prayer. Love is accessed and maintained through prayer. Prayer is your telephone line to the Highest, where the emotions can bathe in love, the mind can be enlightened and the soul can be exalted.

TREASURE NUMBER FOUR: *MEDITATION*

"...Meditation, then is prayer, but is prayer from <u>within</u> the <u>inner</u> self, and partakes not only of the physical inner man but the soul that is aroused by the spirit of man from within..."
--Edgar Cayce Reading 281-13

In vocal prayer we lift our voices to God. In meditation, we lift our minds to God. This means quieting the mind so it can be open to God. Getting an active mind to become silent is more than some students can handle. Nevertheless, acquiring this ability is worth more than gold. Inner peace and strength come from attunement with the spiritual force within. Mystics refer to meditation as "re-fueling at the Cosmic fount." Some have even hinted that this is where the fountain of youth is found.

While we have several types of meditation to choose from, I have selected a meditation that will quiet the body and help you find peace of mind. But first, let's go over a simple but powerful breathing and protection exercise.

BREATHING EXERCISE

Begin by finding a quiet, comfortable place where you can be alone. Then allow your thoughts to drift through your consciousness as if they were clouds; just let them float away into the sky.

Through class experience, I have found that breathing exercises help students to relax and prepare for meditation, as follows:

<u>Inhale</u> slowly and deeply and think: *I am inbreathing the golden quality of peace.*

Keep holding your breath in, while silently saying: *I am absorbing the golden quality of peace.*

<u>Exhale</u> slowly and think: *I am expanding the golden quality of peace.*

Continue holding your breath out while thinking: *I am projecting the golden quality of peace.*

Repeat this exercise two or three times, until you are quiet and relaxed.

Certain breathing exercises provide a way for you to feel energized and to draw in desired qualities such as peace, love, harmony and joy. Eons ago, mankind breathed in longer rhythms, rather than the short breaths we take now. Therefore, it is beneficial to use the above breathing exercise with deeper, longer breaths. This enables the physical body to take in more of the prana, or vital essence, needed for energy.

After you have established a relaxing rhythm of breathing, you might want to create an aura of protection to screen out unwanted interference. I like to think of using this protection as a busy executive uses his secretary to screen unwanted interruptions.

THE PROTECTION EXERCISE

In the beginning, when humanity first made its appearance on earth, we had a natural aura of pure, white essence surrounding the outer, physical body. But through misuse of the original God-energy, we lost this protective shield. As an aid on the path to mastery, I strongly urge that you perform this exercise before beginning any intuitive or spiritual activity, such as meditation. In addition, you may also choose to do this upon awakening, before stepping out of your home, before driving a car or flying in an airplane. It can also help you cope with adversity, crime, violence or negative thoughts coming from others, such as jealousy, and power plays in work situations.

(1) Still the mind and body. Visualize your individualized Presence of God about fifteen feet above your head. This is what the Eastern religions refer to as the "oversoul." This part of yourself is without blemish; it is the spiritual self that is connected to God. It is a pure white essence that envelopes your body when you call upon it, as in the decree below in this oversoul is always present, but very few can see it with the physical eye because it vibrates at a higher speed than we normally can perceive. People who are able

42

to perceive vibrations above the normal range, such as clairvoyants or adepts, can see the oversoul. With practice, you will eventually become aware of it. (This is the light that Earl saw above me that night in the restaurant, in Treasure Number One. Earl and I were drawn together for a spiritual lesson. He had developed extra-sensory perception to the level where he became aware of higher vibrations. But he needed me to cement this reality, and I needed him to confirm my ability in psychometry.)

(2) Call on the Presence through a decree, as follows:

Pillar of Light Decree

"I call on the I AM Presence of God to surround me with a tube of dazzling white light substance, like sun glistening snow, pouring down around me as a circular wall of light; this light essence is constantly pouring like Niagara Falls." (See this tube to be about nine feet in diameter and three feet thick. One becomes that upon which he concentrates. Since all things have originated from the light, light brings perfection and control of all things.)

On October 26, 1990, I received permission from A.D.K. Luk to share this and other decrees from her books. She is author of *Law of Life* and *Law of Life Decrees.* In her letter she wrote:

"The white light for protection is not just a wall of light. Most people do not know how to visualize, and it should be simple for them to begin. That protection to be drawn forth is a pillar of Light. It is not hollow in the center; it is light substance all the way through, and you stand in that like standing in a large searchlight. But the outside, one can think of it as a crust, impenetrable to anything not of light—divine love."

This may cause you to ask: What is a *decree*? The dictionary describes it as an edict promulgated by authority; one of the eternal purposes of God, by which events are foreordained. Decrees were given an importance in the Bible: "Thou shalt decree a thing, and it shall be established unto thee, and upon thy ways the light shall shine."   (Job, 22:28)

Decrees are recognized as powerful instruments for physical manifestations of spiritual law, or precipitation. In a later chapter, we will develop this further.

One day I received a telephone call from Gina, one of my students.

"Mary," she said, "I have a woman at my home who needs help. I know you can explain the white light of protection to her better than I can.

"Put her on the line," I told her.

The woman was undergoing enormous stress caused by a teenage son who threatened to kill her. She had been divorced, and was trying to perform the parental duties of both father and mother. But the son was rebelling against her. I went into detail about the white light of protection and gave her the protection decree to use. She tried this, and within a week she called back to say she was mystified by how this had greatly improved conditions at home. The son was more subdued and had stopped threatening her. As I had suggested, she was envisioning the light of protection around herself, as well as around her son.

Another student sent me a note about her experience with the protection:

"I thought you might be interested in knowing that I had an opportunity to share some of what I have learned with my friend in South America. I left the teachings on the white light with her. She is using this to heal her daughter. Unfortunately, there is a lot of negativity in her house. Also, by using the white light before my plane trip and the meditation you gave me, I was less nervous during the flight, which was very rough."

A MEDITATION EXERCISE

Now that we have established a method for becoming quiet and relaxed, with a protection exercise to screen out unwanted activity, we are ready to go into meditation.

(Students have found it helpful to put these exercises on audio tape, then play them back when they are ready to meditate.)

Situate yourself in a chair in a comfortable atmosphere. Go through the breathing exercises, and the protection exercise with the decree. Close your eyes. Focus your attention on the space between the eyebrows. Imagine yourself looking at a still pond, upon which you may see mental images or pictures. You may hear someone talking to you, as a voice on a radio. Enjoy the peace that is your heritage. Say to yourself, "I am at peace." Take a few minutes to dwell in that peace. If, for some reason, your mind is not ready yet, just keep thinking, "I am at peace." Soon you will be able to quiet the mind and feel at peace. Eastern meditators find it effective to repeat a single word, or *mantra*, such as the primal sound, "Ohm," to get them into a deeper state of consciousness. Think about a goal you are attempting to achieve, such as improving your memory, or reducing stress. If your mind wanders, that's all right. But if you want to bring it to a more meditative state, repeat, "I am at peace," or "Ohm," and soon you will get deeper into it.

During meditation we have the opportunity to tap the power of intuition and surrender ourselves to the Divine within. Allow yourself at least fifteen minutes to meditate. Then bring to mind a friend who is in need of help; say a short prayer for him or her. This way you are sharing the blessings you receive while in meditation. After meditation, the body and mind may return to activity with more freshness, awareness and creativity.

Pat yourself on the back for taking the time to do something good for yourself. The blessings you receive are simply immeasurable, according to Maharishi Mahesh Yogi. Since the 1960s, he has taught a Transcendental Meditation Program to such luminaries as the Beatles and Shirley MacLaine. This program includes a natural technique to accomplish a state of deep rest. The TM program is practiced for approximately 20 minutes, twice a day, preferably in the morning and evening. During this time the body and mind relaxes, while silently repeating a mantra. Studies indicate that this type of level of rest can be deeper than sleep.

Research has attributed many benefits to meditation such as: improved health, better relationships, increased learning and memory abilities, better job performance, reduction of stress, migraines, anxiety and depression, normalization of blood pressure and reduced use of alcohol, cigarettes and drugs.

Dr. Robert Keith Wallace of the University of California Los Angeles (UCLA) selected college students who had been practicing Transcendental Meditation from six months to three years, for twenty minutes daily in the morning and evening. This is what his research found:

1) <u>Decrease in Oxygen Consumption</u>. Metabolic rate is obtained by measuring oxygen consumption. During Transcendental Meditation, oxygen consumption decreases. The decrease in metabolic rate was deeper and occurred faster than during sleep. This is a natural physiological change due to a lowered requirement of oxygen by the cells. One application that developed from this was the use of Transcendental Meditation by astronauts during long space travel to reduce their consumption of oxygen, anxiety and stress.

2) <u>Cardiac Output</u>. The flow of blood volume per unit of time decreased by twenty-five percent. The heart rate diminished by five beats per minute. There was normalization of high blood pressure.

3) <u>Blood Lactate</u>. The ionized lactic acid salt particles in the blood decreased by fifty percent. Since increase in lactate goes with attacks in anxiety, the reduction meant less anxiety during meditation.

4) <u>Galvanic Skin Response</u>. The resistance of the skin to the passing of an electrical current through it increased by 500 percent. There was less tension and the palms of the hands had less sweat.

Further research was conducted after the results of the above experiments:

1) <u>Drug Treatment</u>. Dr, Herbert Benson of Harvard University School of Medicine suggested Transcendental Meditation to some of his patients suffering from high blood pressure.

These patients had been addicted to such drugs as marijuana, barbituates, L.S.D. and heroin. All of the patients who practiced Transcendental Meditation gave up drugs and told Dr. Benson that since meditating, they had found drugs distasteful.

2) <u>Reduced Use of Alcohol and Cigarettes</u>. A study of 1,862 subjects who had practiced Transcendental Meditation for an average of twenty months showed a significant reduction in the use of alcohol and cigarettes. I can personally confirm the matter of cigarettes. Within six months of practicing Transcendental Meditation, I found myself smoking less and less without even thinking about it. Finally, one day I realized that I was only smoking one cigarette a day, plus I did not really enjoy smoking anymore. At that moment I decided that if I could reduce my smoking to one cigarette a day, I could quit smoking forever. It has been over twenty years since I have smoked, and my health has benefited from it.

3) <u>Increased   Job   Satisfaction.</u>   Subjects   practicing Transcendental Meditation for an average of eleven months showed a greater increase in job satisfaction than nonmeditators. High level executives showed a greater increase than lower level employees who meditated. Perhaps this is because executives have more opportunities to use creativity than lower level employees. However, with the continuous practice of meditation, any person can glean the results of becoming more creative. Meditators find ways to improve on what they are doing on their jobs, or become more confident to look for a more meaningful position. It is truly amazing to follow up on an idea that was received during meditation and then see it manifest as something productive.

TREASURE NUMBER FIVE:
CONTEMPLATION

"When concentration, meditation, and superconscious perception are simultaneous, this is perfect contemplation, As a result of the mastery of perfect contemplation the light of direct knowledge dawns in the mind. Perfect contemplation should be practiced to experience ever higher states of consciousness ."

--YOGA SUTRAS 3:4-6

Contemplation is a deeper form of meditation. We go beyond lifting our minds to God; we lift our hearts and expand our innermost essence. Any form of prayer involving the heart and love is contemplation. When a thought comes into the consciousness from the heart, it brings a feeling of peace upon contemplation. The activity of thought and contemplation from the heart is the springboard to knowledge of the Truth. With the heart we see what is truly important, but invisible to the eyes.

When you are uncertain about any life issue, go to the center of your heart and ask the question. Listen for the answer. When truth presents itself through a lecture or book, a feeling in your heart will make you sit up and listen. Through your heart you will recognize the truth when it appears. God's voice is not always heard through words, but often through a feeling in the heart.

A great example of contemplation comes from the life of Prince Siddhartha Guatama, the son of a king in India about the sixth century B.C. He married Princess Yasodhra and had a son. Siddhartha led a protected life within the palace walls until he became curious and secretly ventured out into the streets. After seeing a man begging for food, he became very distressed to learn that people lived in poverty. Disillusioned by the sudden destruction of all he had assumed about life, he left his family, inheritance, and position to go out into the world in search of truth.

After six years of living an austere life as a hermit, Siddhartha entered into contemplation. He raised himself through ever-higher states of consciousness and into the eternal light of God to become a master of vibration, energy and consciousness. This led him to become the fullness of love. When he attained illumination and was transfigured, he earned the titles of "The Enlightened One" and "Buddha." He walked the country of India, teaching the truth by word and example for forty-five years.

You can move into the fullness of love through spiritual knowledge. If you don't know how to integrate love and meditation, here is a short, simple exercise which has produced positive results for students:

SUNSHINE EXERCISE

Visualize the sun. See the sun as a golden-white light above your head. The light showers its protection in, through and around you. Next, envision the sun sending down a delicate pink ray, reaching the top of your head and filling your heart area. Inhale to the count of 4, then exhale to the count of 11. As you breathe in, visualize the sun over your head. As you breathe out, visualize the pink ray descending upon you, entering the top of your head and continuing down to the heart area. Inhale again as you are aware of the pink ray above you; exhale to see its ray flow down and fill you again. Get in touch with that ray of love. Feel centered in its warmth. Find the area of silence and peace within your heart. Feel the love that flows out from the center of your being. Let flow a soft glow that surrounds you with a misty caress. Bask in the light ray of love in complete silence. Think of yourself as floating in space, where all is quiet, surrounded by love and light. After a minimum of five minutes, bring yourself back to earth and your contemplation area, bringing the feeling of love with you.

As you go through your day, radiate this light of love to those with whom you come into contact.

Some scientists may tell you that the brain is the most important organ of the body, but what would you say?

The heart is the most important organ of the body, because the center of life is the heart. And if consciousness does not reside in the heart, it eventually dies.

Those who desire to develop spiritually must learn to think with the heart. The heart, the central power, must be at peace with itself and the whole body. When this happens, peace rules and registers itself in the countenance of the person by an attractive angelic radiance. Kindliness and peacefulness always produce beauty, giving the face a touch of heaven, because beauty is the light of the soul reflected in the forms of matter. But don't just take my word on why thinking with the heart is important. Here is what Dr. Christiane Northrup has to say about it in her newsletter, Health Wisdom for Women, April, 1996:

"Research at the Institute of Heart Math (IHM) has shown that the heart is far more than a mechanical pump. In fact, its electromagnetic field profoundly influences your ability to process information. When the electrical patterns of the brain are synchronized with the electrical patterns of the heart, more intelligence and intuition become available to your brain. Though almost everyone knows that the brain produces electrical activity in the form of brain waves, few realize that the electrical activity of the heart (heart waves) is 40 to 60 times stronger than that of the brain. In fact, the electromagnetic field of the heart can be measured several feet away from your body. And IHM research has shown that sincere experiences of appreciation, joy and caring ('heartfelt emotions') bring about increased coherence in the electromagnetic field of your heart—and in the hearts of those around you. This increased coherence also balances hormonal patterns so that a sense of well-being is generated throughout your entire system."

It has always been advantageous to set aside quiet time in order to focus on spiritual concepts that help us to know God better. In order to love God and God's ways, we need to have spiritual knowledge, for knowledge precedes love. Time spent on increasing our knowledge of spiritual concepts renews the mind and spirit. I suggest reading the Holy Bible, or some other inspirational book, then reflecting on what message it is bringing to you. God's words of love can fill our hearts and minds, plus transform our worries through our contemplation of His Word.

After reading for a few minutes, allow time for reflection. Ask yourself: What have I read? What lesson does it teach me? How have I acted in regard to this subject until now? What shall I do about it in the future? How can this enhance my life?

One biblical verse often puzzled me. Then one day I had the opportunity to glean more understanding. It was during a weekend program at the Yoga Meditation Center in Rochester, New York, where a yogi from India was the featured speaker.

My heart jumped when the yogi said, "The kingdom of God is within you." That was the verse which had puzzled me!

At the afternoon break, I approached him. I asked, "How do we find the kingdom of God within?"

His eyes were large and alight with fire as he said, "The Master Jesus attributed His healing powers to the Father within the kingdom that was within Himself. Some teachings state that the kingdom is within the heart. Do you think this means the physical heart?"

I was thoughtful for a moment. "I guess so."

"We are not just talking about a physical organ, but something deeper within our interior."

"Then how do we get to this interior?" I inquired.

"The opening to our interior being is through a state of consciousness…an inner sanctuary that can be reached only through one door. And that door is controlled by the Overself.

"The Overself is your spiritual self, the <u>real</u> you. Try to see your Overself as a connection to the Universal Godhead. There is a silver cord that originates from the Godhead and is connected to the Overself. From the Overself the cord goes through your head and is anchored in the heart. Within the physical heart is an inner chamber that contains the flame of everlasting life. The inner chamber of your heart is the opening to the kingdom. It is the door which admits you to Divine Consciousness."

"But how do I open the door?"

"Through contemplation. By going consciously within the heart, you discover that you are not separate, but one with a higher consciousness. You discover that which seemed separate in the outer world was only reflection, darkened by lack of understanding. Your lack of understanding has kept you from seeing the precious treasures of the inner world of spirit. Nothing in the outer, material world can compare to these treasures."

"How often should I enter into contemplation?"

"Set aside some time every day to enter into your heart, the Secret Place of the Most High. Feel the connection between your outer self and the inner chamber, focusing your attention on the heart center, visualizing it as a Golden Sun. Then see yourself on an altar of golden light that radiates several feet about you. Let your adoration flow upward to the I AM Presence of God. As your adoration flows to that Presence, know that your body is the temple of the Immortal Flame of Eternal Life, awaiting your adoration and love. Say, with deep reverence, that God is in this Holy Temple.

"By thinking, acting and speaking as the Master Jesus or Buddha would do, you gain entrance to the electrical power of I AM Consciousness. The door is kept closed until the awakened one makes an effort to find the true source of life. There is only one pure motive that opens the door—the desire to serve God within you and within every human being. When this becomes the primary motive of your life, then Divine Love surges through the cord to welcome you into the Kingdom. This comes after a period of testing to see if you can be distracted by outer worldly allurements. After you pass the test, your soul and mind are enlightened, your heart is aflame, and your lamp is lit. You will experience a tremendous joy that no one can take away from you."

"And one more thing," he said as his right hand went up in the air. "The soul of the mystic passes through stages of purification and illumination, from worldly knowledge to intuitive knowledge. As the soul reaches the stage of perfection, a light dawns on the soul, revealing the hidden mysteries of the Godhead. Through this, the soul is carried away from this visible world, becoming intoxicated with the wine of the love of God, experiencing an ecstasy with the ability to look upon the Divine Essence. This keeps the soul from being drawn away to the baser things of life.

"Always remember that such glimpses of the Divine need to be of short duration; otherwise the soul may be unwilling to return to the lower vibrations of the earth plane."

So that was how I came to understand "The kingdom of God is within you."

SECTION SUMMARY

In our quest for a peaceful life, we have the following tools at our disposal: Prayer, meditation, and contemplation. Prayer allows us to enjoy a special relationship with God and our own higher self. Once we learn to quiet our mind and body, and use a protective technique, we can rest within a tranquil security that tells us we are never alone.

These three tools can help us find a balance between our physical and spiritual needs. A commitment to these activities brings our inner self to a place of peace. Then we are able to communicate in a more meaningful way with the Infinite and apply the messages we perceive to our behavior in the outside world.

Through intuition, prayer, meditation and contemplation, we are building a bridge between us and God…a bridge to freedom. We need to develop the faculty of intuition because it is through this faculty that we can discern the reality of God. Discernment keeps our minds, awareness and consciousness clarified. All three of these practices of prayer, meditation and contemplation provide opportunities for Self- and God-Realization. You will find that once a peaceful interior world is firmly established, your inner peace spills over to different areas of your life. You can expand it to your outer environment, to your entire household, and generate a positive influence on your family and guests.

Are you interested in how you can make your home a place of peace? Then turn to the next treasure.

SECTION THREE: MAKING YOUR HOME A HAVEN OF PEACE

TREASURE NUMBER SIX: *IMPROVING YOUR SURROUNDINGS*

When there is order in the home, there will be peace in the nation.

--Ancient Chinese Proverb

What does your environment have to do with achieving peace? Many factors in our surroundings exert an influence on our lives. What you choose to include in your home and your workplace—furniture, colors, lighting, accessories, even the people who visit—will have a conscious and subconscious affect on you.

You will discover many benefits in becoming **more aware** of the various components, how they look, and the feelings you derive from having them around. The more consciously you create your environment, the more "at home" you will feel in it.

Conscious means being aware of one's existence, sensations, cognition; awakened. Consequently, the more you are aware or awake to your surroundings, the more you can control what is going on around you. *Subconscious* is existing or operating beneath or beyond consciousness; the totality of the mental processes of which the individual is not aware. *Superconscious* is a state of consciousness superior to the normal states, which allows progressive transformations, leading to cosmic consciousness, or God consciousness.

Your home is a reflection of who you are. What does your home say about you? Is it a place where visitors can feel comfortable? If not, they might produce negative vibrations in your home that you will feel, either consciously or subconsciously.

Whether or not you realize it, your home is an outpicturing of your life. Is it a clean, orderly space, an indicator of an orderly mind? Or is it so cluttered, dirty and messy that guests would be afraid to accept a cup of coffee?

Do you want to have a home where others will feel at ease, or one that will scare them away? The choice is yours. Why not cultivate a place where love can live and grow in harmony, order and peace?

How can you build an environment that will surround you with a sense of peace? This chapter will provide some unique suggestions. First, let's think about cleansing the area so it can be truly your own, and you can have a fresh start from which to begin implementing the ideas I offer.

CLEANSING YOUR HOME

What can you do to cleanse the house of negative vibrations that were left behind by previous homeowners, renters, or unwanted visitors? You already know how to clean your home physically with the vacuum cleaner and mop, but do you know how to cleanse your home spiritually?

Here are a few methods that have been successful:

(1) <u>Sage</u> that grows on a bush in the Southwest has been used by Native Americans in purification ceremonies. When my husband and I moved into our first home, I could still feel the negative energies of the previous owners, a couple who had experienced violent arguments. A friend who lives in New Mexico sent me some fresh sage, which she had picked from a bush, in strands about six inches long, tied with string, and packed in a plastic bag. I was delighted to receive this bouquet that was about one inch in diameter. After I lit the top of the sage bouquet with a match, I watched it smoke like an incense stick. Carrying it from room to room, I blessed each, saying: "Holy Spirit, most pure and powerful, bless and cleanse this room thoroughly." Sage burns slowly and has a clean aroma. It is available at some New Age bookstores. Ask for a "smudge stick." If you can not find it, try burning incense instead--another way to cleanse a room of unwanted energy.

(2) <u>Holy water</u> accomplishes the same thing as sage and is easier to obtain—bring a clean, empty bottle to a Catholic

church and fill it free of charge. A holy-water spigot usually can be found in the vestibule. I have used holy water to bless the homes of people who had problems ranging from feelings of uneasiness to ghost hauntings. Moreover, holy water has been used to ease family problems, sickness, tension and depression. When you say "The Lord's Prayer" while sprinkling the house, room or individual with holy water, the cleansing effect is even greater.

FENG SHUI

When Donald Trump, the New York City real-estate developer, joined with Hong Kong investors to build a city within a city on Manhattan's West Side, one of the stipulations was that this billion-dollar Riverside South project (retail stores, offices, and private living spaces) be planned according to the ancient principles of Feng Shui. This high-powered commercial application is proof that Feng Shui (pronounced *fung shway*), the Eastern art of placement, is becoming ever more popular in our Western culture. Although it dates back to 202 B.C., the time of the Han Dynasty, Feng Shui principles are currently applied in places extending from Hollywood executive offices to Mr. K's restaurant in Washington, D. C.

Undoubtedly, this discipline is viewed with great seriousness in the Far East. The city of Hong Kong itself was laid out following the principles of Feng Shui. Lung King Chuen, a Feng Shui master, designed one of the most advanced buildings in the world, at a price tag of one billion dollars--the headquarters of the Hong Kong and Shanghai Banking Corporation.

Feng Shui literally means "wind and water." The way in which buildings, landscapes, windows, ledges, or corners are laid out, affects how they interact with wind and water. The figurative translation means "vital forces." The Chinese claim we have many more receptors than the five known senses for picking up vibrations from people, places and things. For example, through our intuition, we perceive feelings such as foreboding or well-being.

Often a Feng Shui expert is consulted before construction begins on a home or an office building to ensure the most fortuitous results. The ability to recognize a fortunate or unfortunate site requires well-developed sensitivity, and a trained eye. Individuals can be favorably or unfavorably affected by the placement and surroundings of their offices and homes. Feng Shui experts develop their powers of reception to become keenly aware of messages from the environment. They believe that when one arranges the environment in harmony with the natural order of the universe, then financial prosperity, good health, and happiness will result. Using this criteria, some surroundings are considered luckier than others. For instance, a house situated at the head of a bay helps money to flow in. A house on a point jutting out in the water does not hold money in, as the water flows away from it. Thus, an expert would advise his client against buying the latter property.

Feng Shui covers a large area of uses from building a house, organizing an office, arranging landscaping, setting favorable dates for special occasions, achieving aesthetic design and harmony, not to mention some mystical cures for finances and physical health.

An office or home is considered to have its own ch'i, just like a human body. Ch'i means "cosmic breath" and "human energy." An even flow of ch'i must run through the doorways, halls and rooms. Door size is important to let in the right amount of ch'i. If the doorway is too small, mirrors can be placed around it to enhance its size. If the door is too large, allowing too much ch'i to escape, then wind chimes can be hung to absorb excess energy. Since it is considered unacceptable to see a stairway from the front door, Interior Designer Ron Mann was asked to invent something to conform to Feng Shui ideals for a San Jose, California resident. His answer was an ascending screen of bamboo in front of the stairs, creating an entrance grove effect.

For centuries, the masters of Feng Shui had been able to detect good and harmful spirits as defined by the Chinese religions of Taoism, Buddhism, and Confucianism. These masters carefully evaluate the entrance of a home, which establishes its mood for visitors. Consciously or subconsciously you can sense various feelings every time you enter a home—you may feel light, happy, welcome feelings, or heavy and depressed ones. According to Feng Shui principles, if the entrance restricts the even flow of ch'i, and the energy is withdrawn, the dweller may be self-destructive. If the entrance placement allows the ch'i to flow smoothly, the dweller will enjoy excellent health and good luck.

MYSTICAL HOME-CLEANSING METHOD

Another successful home-cleansing method comes from the Black Hat Sect School, one of the best-known branches of Feng Shui. This housewarming ritual is designed to claim ownership and control of your home or apartment. The Chinese say it chases away negative vibrations or spirits left over from previous residents.

Method: Cut nine lemons or oranges in half and juice them. Take the skins and place them in a large bowl, covering them with water. Let the mixture stand for a couple of hours, then drain the water into a clean atomizer or spray bottle. Squirt the citrus water into each corner of the room—just a short spray. Do this in every room. I used this method myself and was delighted by how peaceful my home felt afterwards.

Are you interested in drawing more prosperity to yourself? One Feng Shui master suggests utilizing every burner on the kitchen stove, instead of using only the front burners. This is symbolic of making use of all resources. Colors also have a great influence on prosperity, as well as achieving harmony.

COLORS

What colors have you chosen for your decor? Think about the colors you have on the walls, curtains, furniture or rugs. Everyone's ch'i reacts to color. Some colors have a soothing effect; others can be irritating. If you want to produce a peaceful or spiritual home environment, notice how certain colors affect you, and choose your colors carefully.

Pat Kerr of Locust Hill, Ontario, Canada, has researched the effect of color on healing. Green, for example, has a healing influence, which is why it has been used in hospitals for many years. Doctors call it a "living" color. Blue is calming, and for that reason airlines choose it for passenger cabins. Since orange increases the appetite, it has been used in restaurants (remember Howard Johnson's?), cafeterias, and grocery stores. Bright red is energizing, while hot pink cools aggressive energies of criminals. In spring, 1997, the police department in Buffalo, New York, painted its jail cells a bright magenta shade. On the other hand, it is recommended that you decorate your bedroom with a soft pink motif for romance and lovemaking.

Use the following list of seven basic colors from the electromagnetic spectrum to aid you in choosing colors for your environment:

RED This color is the vehicle of the physical life force. Red brings physical, cheerful energy. It is a good color to wear when your energy is low, but may be too strong a choice for walls or large areas of the house.

ORANGE Orange is the color of prana, the life force that works with the material mind and is mentally invigorating. It also can lift body temperature and stimulate circulation.

YELLOW This is the color through which spiritual essence manifests. It is considered the soul color and gives a mental boost. Yellow is the color of illumination and wisdom.

GREEN This color is the midpoint link between the physical and spiritual range of color and vibration. It is the color of infinite intelligence. Green can help you to grow spiritually, heal and prosper.

BLUE The light blue color of the sky covers, protects, and spiritualizes. Its effect is uplifting, inspiring, soothing and comforting.

INDIGO This is a dark-blue or sapphire blue, representing the mind power of the spiritual plane, radiating to earth and manifesting through humanity. This is a force of creativity higher than can be reached by using logic and is capable of lifting the mind above human consciousness.

VIOLET Violet color vibrates higher than the physical plane. Its transmuting effect changes the lower elements of the physical plane into the higher elements of the spiritual plane, causing a purifying effect.

To produce a more peaceful effect in your world, opt for soft pastels such as pink, aqua, light blue, white and light green.

MUSIC

What kind of music do you play in your home? As you listen to background music, pay attention to how you are feeling. Is the music soothing, or does it make you tense? If certain rock music has been found to have a negative effect on plants, what do you think it does to your body? Did you know that Beethoven's Fifth Symphony is healing? The great symphonies of Mozart and Bach and any of the Strauss waltzes can be uplifting. When you are looking for harmony, look to music, and allow the sweet-sounding notes to bathe your senses and environment.

Music plays a more important role in life of which individuals may be unaware. The word universe (uni-verse) actually means one song. We are all united in one song, sometimes called the music of the spheres. Music can help us tap into the vibration of universal harmony, as well as relax us. Achieving a deep state of relaxation is possible with soothing music. Music can induce relaxation. When music and relaxation are utilized on a regular schedule, you can reduce stress, improve your immune system and find more ease in falling asleep.

CANDLES AND AROMATHERAPY

Is someone in your home generating a lot of negative energy, such as anger? Are you having a disagreement with your spouse or children? Try lighting a pink candle. It will produce a more loving atmosphere, since, in the study of metaphysics, pink represents love.

Aromatherapy candles are currently hot retail items, purposely scented to produce certain feelings. As the candles burn, an essence of oil is released, which can reduce stress, relieve headaches, or enhance emotional well-being. The flame of a candle can also cleanse the atmosphere of old thought patterns.

Although aromatherapy is an old art and science that was used in ancient Egypt, it is gaining recognition in the modern scientific community. Through inhalation of essential oils--the liquids that are distilled from bushes, trees, roots, seeds, flowers and plants--the sense of smell affects the limbic system, the emotional center of the brain. This is why certain aromas improve emotional health, and stimulate endorphin production. The hormone, endorphin, is a natural opiate which elevates your mood without side effects.

For instance, if you are having a stressful day, try adding a few drops of rose oil to your bath water to produce a sense of euphoria. The essential oil of rose brings harmonic balance to the energy centers of the body, allowing the energy to flow more smoothly throughout the body.

An essential oil called **Peace and Calming** may help to calm overactive children. Simply dip it on a cotton ball and place it in air vents in your home or car. Or you may get a special air pump, called a diffuser, that disburses essential oils in a micro-fine vapor, suspending it into the atmosphere for several hours. Using any essential oil this way can reduce mold, bacteria, or basically freshen the air with fragrance. I have been helped with allergy problems by diffusing an essential oil called **Purification**.

Purification is used to purify the air in the home or work environment. Its essence neutralizes poison from insect bites, mildew, cigarette smoke and other undesirable odors in a home or confined area. You can apply it to affected areas of the skin, or it may be applied behind the ears and on pulse areas to repel insects when you are outdoors. This is a good essential oil to diffuse.

The essential oil, Angelica, has been dubbed the "oil of the angels." It was used in ancient times to increase the aura around the physical body, giving the wearer a feeling of protection. It is beneficial to use with meditation or contemplation because of its soothing effect, and is usually dabbled on the shoulders, forehead, wrists and behind the ears.

An interesting story on the origination of the term, "aromatherapy," reveals that in 1920, a French chemist had an accident in his laboratory. Rene-Maurice Gattefosse, Ph.D., suffered a third-degree burn on his arm and immediately dipped it into a vat of lavender oil, assuming it was water. This caused the burning to stop within minutes. With the continuous application of lavender oil, the burn eventually healed without a scar. After analyzing this essential oil, Dr. Gattefosse concluded that essential oils have special healing qualities and coined the word, aromatherapy. Lavender has become known as the universal oil, because of its wide spectrum of uses. Besides healing burns, it has been known to heal rashes, psoriasis, scarring, headaches and pain. It has helped with insomnia because of its sedative and calming effect.

Robert O. Becker, M.D., author of *The Body Electric*, enlightened me about the electrical frequency of the body. Frequency is a measurable rate of electrical energy flow which is constant between two points. Everything in life has a frequency. I found it astounding that essential oils possess frequencies which are several times greater than the frequencies found in food and herbs. By measuring frequency by hertz, it was discovered that canned food had a hertz frequency of zero. Fresh vegetables and fruits has a frequency of 15 hertz. The frequency of dry herbs ranged from 20 to 27. I was stunned to learn that essential oils started at 52 hertz, all the way up to 320 hertz, the high frequency of rose oil. A healthy body usually has a frequency from 62 to 78 hertz. Therefore, when the frequency gets lower than 62, disease begins. What does all this mean? It means that it is vital to keep our frequencies high enough to avoid disease, and that is possible with essential oils. In addition to that, essential oils can be an invaluable tool toward helping a person's spiritual well-being, as well as physical. The more we raise our frequencies and vibrations, the more we raise our consciousness.

PICTURES AND DECORATIONS

I will never forget what happened when I was visiting a friend's apartment years ago. I froze in horror when I spotted a gruesome picture of Satan staring back at me from the wall. Next to the picture was an end table with a statue of a cobra about to strike. To say that these decorations did not produce an atmosphere of peace is a hilarious understatement.

The eerie glare of the picture and the threatening cobra made me want to run out of apartment as fast as I could go. Do we truly understand the sensitivities of our natural being? Whether we realize it or not, certain negative influences in the environment can have a lingering, uncomfortable subconscious effect.

For your own well-being, move through your living space slowly and evaluate every accessory on display. Remove pictures, statues, and decorations that could be affecting you, your family, or your guests in a negative, unpeaceful way.

One of my students told me that he wanted more than anything else to be in a relationship. Yet when I had occasion to visit his condominium, his walls were decorated with paintings of warriors—lone, stoic, expressionless men. Even the pictures hung alone, rather than in pairs or in groupings. I wondered whether this fellow's consciousness, of which his home was an outpicturing, would allow for a partner?

When I visited the apartment of another student, who is always surrounded by friends and attracts people easily, I saw how her belongings were arranged in pairs and clusters—two paperweights, two chairs and sofa in a conversation group, and so on. This woman's consciousness clearly showed itself in her interior design.

During a stressful experience, a spiritual teacher told me that hanging a picture of a Native American Chief in my home would produce a sense of harmony. At first, this sounded ludicrous, and besides, where would I get such a picture? At the time, Native American pictures were not as popular as they are today. But fate stepped in to take me into the office of my supervisor.

It turned out that he disliked a picture of a Sioux Chief which was hanging behind his desk. I was flabbergasted when he asked, "Would you like to take this picture home? It was left behind by the man I replaced, and I'd rather have it out of here." Thoughts of my spiritual teacher went through my mind, and I accepted the offer. After hanging the picture in the dining room, I noticed that family members were more calm than they had been in months. And guess what the bonus was? It was a painting by Frederic Remington, famous for his portrayal of the American West.

Pictures have a tremendous influence on children, so choose carefully the types of pictures that your children will view. Wood brings warmth and security to a child's room. Light wood provokes a very positive response, as well as reddish and toned woods, such as mahogany. Black wood disturbs the nervous system. Avoid bare, dull walls which have a disturbing effect on the emotions of a sensitive child. For the benefit of your child, keep in mind that children's feelings are formed by their surroundings.

FLOWERS AND PLANTS

Have you ever wondered why the Creator gave us flowers, one of His miracles? Flowers not only produce beauty with their appearance, but also with their color and fragrance. My home in New York State had a garden with a variety of flowers blooming from spring until fall. When the fragrant Symphony roses were in bloom, I would take some to my office. The gesture elevated the atmosphere among my colleagues who were happy to receive those delicate pink roses.

Flowers promote positive energy, good feelings and can give a look of warmth or dignity to an environment. After picking lilacs off the bushes during the month of May, the pleasant aroma pervaded the whole house as they sat on a table in a vase. Not only did I feel good, but my visitors enjoyed the fragrance and feeling in the air.

Flowers also have mystical healing properties. A few years ago, I brought magnolias to a neighbor who was in the hospital.

When I walked into her room with those fragrance blooms, her face lit up with happiness. She later told me that whenever she felt depressed about her illness, she would gaze at the flowers and become uplifted with their beauty and distinctive aroma. All this from just a few white flowers!

Plants have a special influence, too, because they give off oxygen and purify the air. Many plants—evergreens, for example—have the healthful color of green, and infuse the room with pleasant aromas. The scent of pine is conducive to peaceful meditations.

SETTING UP A SACRED PLACE

The act of designating a special place in your home for prayer or meditation has a beneficial effect on the subconscious mind, because the subconscious reacts favorably to routine and designated spaces. That is why I advise setting aside a sacred place, such as an altar or prayer table, in your home. On this small table or desk, place any objects that you consider sacred. You might include prayer cards, a prayer list, a rosary, candles, incense, holy books—such as the Bible or Bhagavad-Gita (the timeless epic of the Hindu faith)—or statues. You may wish to include mementos, such as rocks or dried wildflowers from a particularly memorable walk in the woods, photographs of loved ones, or something inherited from a relative who has passed away.

For meditating, set aside an area that is quiet and private, with your favorite chair, cushions, tape recorder, and whatever else you may use for that sacred time. By going to that specific, quiet place every day, your mind will be conditioned to become still.

A sacred place might also be an outdoor garden—an herb garden or butterfly garden.

Lynn, a woman who attended one of my workshops, told me about her method of finding peace. After her husband passed away, she found it difficult to get up in the morning. Her depression got worse every day. Finally, the idea came to her to create a butterfly garden in her yard.

Lynn carefully designed her garden with nectar-producing flowers to attract butterflies to host plants. She had learned that each species of butterfly goes to a host plant for egg laying and nurturing their resulting caterpillars.

Then Lynn organized a meditation area within the garden, adding the touch of certain stones and chairs. When it was all completed, she found she had a special place to go after she awakened each morning. She couldn't wait to get outdoors to watch the butterflies change life forms from the larva to the chrysalis to the free-winged beauty. It gave her something to look forward to each day. To her, this metamorphosis was proof that life never really dies; it only changes from one form to another. The garden gave Lynn renewed faith in the process of life.

I close this treasure of "Improving Your Surroundings" with a pearl of wisdom from the man known as "The Sleeping Prophet," Edgar Cayce:

"In the establishing of the home, make it as that which may be the pattern of a heavenly home. Not as that set aside for only a place to sleep or to rest, but where not only self but all who enter there may feel, may experience, by the very vibrations that are set up by each in the sacredness of the home, a helpfulness, a hopefulness in the air about the home....Make thine home, thine abode, where an angel would desire to visit, where an angel would seek to be guest."

--Edgar Cayce Reading 480-20

TREASURE NUMBER SEVEN: *PERSONAL RELATIONSHIPS*

"Keep the fires of love burning in thy hearts day by day, for the love of God is manifested in the earth through those that are just kind to one another.

Be patient, be kind. Be gentle in thy ministerings day by day; for though there may come those periods when the burden seems heavy, and the light fades in the life, yet he that is faithful unto the end shall wear the crown."

--Edgar Cayce Reading 281-16

The previous treasure unfolded environmental aspects for the home. Now we shall focus on an aspect concerning significant others—personal relationships.

Each relationship can be challenging. Relationships have a purpose in reflecting who we were when we entered into the relationship and who we are presently. Thus, relationships can help us look at what we are creating in the present and what we created in the past—all through strong thoughts and desires. Through strong desires and prayer we can also bring about changes for improvement.

I have witnessed such changes in students in my classes. Many experience personal growth from attitude and behavioral changes. And some will grow beyond their mate, creating a change in the relationship.

One morning, June, one of my students, called me on the telephone. She sounded desperate and asked if she could come right over to my house. Within thirty minutes, she was standing on my doorstep. I had never seen her in such an emotional state.

June told me that her husband had fits of rage and anger, and she could not tolerate his behavior any longer. She had reached the end of her rope.

June had made great progress in my self-awareness classes. However, it caused her husband to rebel. She no longer expended the same amount of energy to act out the old, familiar patterns when he acted badly.

When June had married Joe, she had been shy and had low self-esteem. Now that she was more self-confident, her response to problems had changed. As she moved into more peace with herself, she no longer needed validation from Joe as to who she was or what she should be. By loving herself more, there was a difference in what she would allow to happen in her life. She was not willing to stand by and watch Joe throw dishes and upset the whole household.

As we sat at my dining room table, I asked June to think about what she had been praying for or creating through strong thoughts. June said she had been praying for a change for the better in her marriage because she still loved her husband. I pointed out that her prayers have been half-answered; only her half of the partnership had changed. Consequently, she was in a relationship that was not matched in energy. She did not want to get caught in the distortion of Joe's actions. Nor did she want to leave him. Therefore, June had another option to explore: to help Joe change the unwanted, unconstructive energy. I gave her instructions on how to use the transmuting violet flame, a decree taken from Ascended Master Teachings.

According to Coptic and Upanishad tenets, these teachings were given only to individuals called *initiates.* An initiate is one who has been admitted into the knowledge of a secret study, and who qualified to receive higher spiritual instructions. Certain initiates were sequestered in faraway retreats or monasteries and trained in ancient wisdom by members of the Brotherhood of Light, such as the Brotherhood of the Essenes. Presently, the consciousness of humanity has risen to such a level that the Ascended Master Teachings may be given to a greater number of people. Individuals who are ready to receive these instructions will be drawn to people or places where they can obtain them, as June was drawn to me for help, and as I had been drawn to my spiritual mentors.

The transmuting violet flame decree (to *transmute* is to bring to a higher state) helps us change negative energy that we have accumulated in the force field around us. It can also be used to change negative energy coming from others.

As this decree is spoken with feeling and visualized in the mind, a transmutation of present negativity is changed into a purified substance. Because we have tarnished our bodies through the years from negative thinking and habits, the energies have to be transmuted to help each individual achieve the God-given right to perfection. The violet flame can dissolve past mistakes and transmute flaws into perfection. It is the door to mastery of your thoughts, feelings, destiny, or whatever you wish to master on earth. The violet flame can be used to transmute depression, irritation, anger, disease, bad habits or any limitation. It can also be used to control your feelings or those of another.

The science of physics has taught us that light is not one-dimensional. To prove this to yourself, all you have to do is observe sunlight as it shines through a white crystal. The spectrum of light is made up of red, orange, yellow, green, blue, indigo, and violet. Each color possesses a different spiritual quality. Violet has the quality of transmutation—healing, purifying energy that brings about positive change—and that is why the flame is visualized in that color.

Here is how to call forth the violet flame:

TRANSMUTING VIOLET FLAME DECREE
"Beloved I AM Presence of God, blaze through and around me the Transmuting Violet Flame, Thy Sacred Fire. Purify and transmute now all impure desires, hard feelings, wrong concepts, imperfect etheric records, causes, cores, effects and memories, known or hidden. Keep this flame sustained and all-powerfully active. Replace all by pure substance, power of accomplishment and the Divine Plan fulfilled."

Repeat this decree three times to help anchor it in your consciousness. Mentally visualize a soothing violet flame penetrating your whole being. See it blazing under your feet, through all cells of the body, up to a spot above your head.

You will find it helpful to get into the practice of saying the Transmuting Violet Flame Decree every day. This way you will learn it well enough to say it from memory and be able to say it silently whenever a person is out of control.

Some individuals find it helpful to visualize a flame burning in a fireplace, seeing its color as violet or purple. Try to feel joy and comfort, which will make you feel lighter. Hold the visualization for a few minutes to enjoy the full feeling of it. Often students ask if you have to see this with your physical eyes. The answer is no. You can begin the effect by thinking it and seeing it in your mind's eye. By thinking, feeling and saying the decree you bring it into reality. With daily use you will feel the violet flame purify your mind, body and everyday life.

When you feel unhappiness or negativity of any kind, feel the violet flame flash up through you feet to the heart area, where it is purified and changed into a golden flame of peace. See this golden flame blaze through the other person or condition causing your distress. Several weeks later, June reported to me that the Violet Flame Decree had been powerful in calming her husband, as well as calming herself. Their relationship was turned around for the betterment of the whole family.

Why is a flame visualized, rather than a white cloud enclosing the infuriated individual? We use a flame because it symbolizes energy and light. Personal happiness is based on something simple, yet powerful—our ability to invoke light. Our true essence is spiritual light, and every person is using light at every moment; the Light of God sustains our life energy.

We can call forth more light by bringing our attention to it through spiritual attunement. By concentrating on the light, you draw more light to yourself and increase the I AM Presence of God in your world. The Law of Creation is: What you think and feel, you bring into form...whatever your attention is on, you become. Therefore, if your attention is on disappointment, poverty or hate, you will attract and manifest those conditions. If your focus is on contentment, prosperity or love, they are what you bring to your life. Love attracts love. Hate attracts hate.

Similarly, we are forgiven in the same manner that we forgive others. Resentments block us from attaining higher levels of consciousness. The subconscious mind needs to be cleared of anger and grudges in order to move forward in consciousness and spirituality. As you advance on the spiritual path, anything negative which you think, say, or do will come back to you quickly, so that you can transmute it and be free of it. By forgiving those who have committed wrongs against us, we literally leap forward in our spiritual development.

FORGIVENESS AFFIRMATION

Search your memory for individuals who have hurt you. Most people do not have to look too long to accomplish this. On the other hand, you may have consciously forgotten an incident, but your subconscious mind may be harboring the hurt or resentment; so spend time in an attempt to retrieve suppressed memories.

Some of my students have found it helpful to say the following statement for those they need to forgive, until they feel that a change has taken place, or a heavy load has been lifted. This can take anywhere from one to six weeks. Think of the person's name that you need to forgive and say:

"(The person's name), you are a child of God, as I am. I forgive you. I release you. I thank you for all the lessons that you have helped me to learn. I forgive myself. I let go of this pattern of imperfection. I see us only as channels of perfection. Realizing that our highest good is manifesting from this relationship, I abide in peace."

This statement will work wonders, even though you may never see the person again. This is an affirmation to activate the Law of Forgiveness. If you have no particular person to forgive, you may say a more general affirmation in the form of the following decree. Because of the gift of free will, the I AM Presence of God needs to receive our call before giving assistance. When you call upon the I AM Presence of God for forgiveness of all the mistakes that you and all mankind have ever made, you request assistance from God for yourself and for those who are not yet awakened or able to make the call for themselves:

LAW OF FORGIVENESS DECREE

"I call on the I AM Presence of God and the Law of Forgiveness for myself and all mankind to forgive all mistakes, misqualified energy, and for straying from the light. Transmute this misqualified energy into the Light of God that never fails."

Every particle of life entrusted to you must be harmonized, purified and qualified with perfection as it was when it was first given to you. The Law of Forgiveness Decree and the Transmuting Violet Flame Decree will enable you to do this. These two decrees are especially effective when used together because the pure nature of the violet flame is the feeling of forgiveness and mercy. With the practice and application of decrees, you can work out problems of forgiveness, mistakes, uncontrolled emotions, or anything in life you wish to master.

SACRED HALF-HOUR EXERCISE

One day I received a telephone call from my friend, Marty, from Philadelphia.

"I felt an impulse to call," he said. "Are you OK?"

"As a matter of fact," I told him, "I have this empty feeling...as if something is missing."

"Well, I can suggest something that brought fulfillment in my life when I felt like you do now. Want to fill that emptiness?"

"You bet I do!"

"Begin the day with a half-hour of prayer. I know that thirty minutes may seem like a lot of time, but the results are worth every minute. This golden nugget was given to me when I was a supervising engineer for the government. The employees assigned to me were not meeting their deadlines. I was really stressed out until my pastor convinced me to fit a sacred half-hour into my schedule. The pastor reminded me that I was only giving God a few minutes of my time. He said that if I gave God something meaningful that takes effort, God would give me something meaningful back.

"It takes commitment to set thirty minutes aside for God," Marty continued, "but it has helped me solve many problems. I motivated the engineers to the extent that we won an outstanding award! Even though I am retired now, I <u>still</u> start my day with the sacred half-hour of prayer. And I think it has improved my health. My doctor can't believe how healthy I am for my age. Sometimes it takes a challenging event to make us realize that only God can fill the emptiness in our hearts."

I decided to try Marty's suggestion. The next morning, my alarm went off a half-hour earlier, and I headed for the family room. As I sat in my favorite chair, I thought about God and realized that our relationship was not as close as it used to be. I wanted to change that; this was my opportunity.

My thoughts wandered to a problem with an acquaintance. I reached for the Forgiveness Affirmation and the Law of Forgiveness Decree. After saying them, I was given an inspiration on how to deal with the problem in a positive way. Other thoughts came to mind—some were important, some not. My mind felt as if a stagnant puff of smoke was being cleared out. Then I said a prayer I used to say as a child. I felt young again. A pink light enveloped me, and a warm feeling of love vibrated from my head to my toes. I felt the peace and love of God, a new closeness.

By this time my husband's alarm sounded. My quiet period of peace and love had been completed for that morning. I breezed through the day with newfound hope. My problem with the acquaintance was solved beautifully, and I whispered, "Thank you, God!"

SECTION SUMMARY

In Sections One and Two, we learned methods for creating inner peace. In Section Three, we turned our skills to the outer world—the important and immediate environment of our home.

If we cannot be at peace where we live, where <u>can</u> we feel secure and at ease?

The point of this section is to help you consciously create a loving space at home, first by being aware that subtle influences in your home can help create peace or rob you of it. After you have cleansed your home spiritually of any unwelcome energy, analyze all elements of decoration—the colors, pictures, accessories, plants, flowers, and furniture placement. Even the music you select has an effect on peace. Think about the wondrous experiences that can be yours when you create a sacred area in a bedroom, den or garden.

More challenging than interior design are personal relationships. You can transmute negativity, resolve conflicts, and forgive mistakes or hurts through decrees and forgiveness. The more you bring the presence of God into your home, the more you can find treasure and pleasure in your home environment.

Many of my students report that their primary source of stress is their place of employment. Is it possible to bring spiritual harmony to the office, store or factory environments? You will find the answer in the next section.

SECTION FOUR: BRINGING PEACE INTO YOUR WORKPLACE

TREASURE NUMBER EIGHT: *IMPROVING RELATIONSHIPS WITH COLLEAGUES*

He that would have peace and harmony must create and make peace in self and in the relationships with others.
--Edgar Cayce Reading 349—17

The work environment of most organizations is stressful. The causes can be deadlines, bad morale, competitors, restructuring...the list goes on. Is it possible to transform such a space into a place where you can walk in gentle peace? The answer is yes, and you can implement positive changes using two methods: first, by taking steps to improve your relationships with colleagues or co-workers, and second, by making physical adjustments in your surroundings.

At many times during my corporate career, I wondered if I were in a secret training course for dealing with difficult people. This began to surface when management sent me to work with a man whom everyone disliked. He was so obnoxious that a co-worker gave him a nickname to lend humor to a terrible situation. The nickname was Highpockets, because the man used to wear his trousers with suspenders that brought the pants up almost to his armpits.

Why, I pondered, was I unlucky enough to get stuck in an office with a man who drove people crazy? I detested being with him, but I was going to be his associate for a while. I decided to explore my options: (1) I could give up by quitting my job or requesting a transfer, (2) I could resent the situation and become bitter and miserable, or (3) I could create a solution.

I could not get a transfer and could not afford to quit. Nor did I want to become a resentful, bitter person. So I decided to find a creative solution that would transform the problem into an opportunity.

My intuition led me to consult my Spiritual Science studies. I remembered reading that if we could see the divinity, the God-quality in other people, then we could help to bring it out in them, even if they were not experiencing it in their actions. The lessons stated that some individuals need help from others to manifest the good that is within. "Well," I thought, "the divinity is certainly obscure in Highpockets. So how am I going to bring out the good in him?"

For some reason, Will Rogers, Oklahoma cowboy, philosopher, and humorist, came to mind. He had written a weekly newspaper that was read by over a million Americans. From his popular vaudeville act, he went to Hollywood to become the number-one box-office attraction in 1934. One of his famous quotes was: "I never met a man I didn't like." Will Rogers must have found a way to see the good in others.

I was determined to learn how to see the good in others. My inner guidance led me to some material on the teachings of the Masters of the Far East.

The lessons showed a drawing of the overself, which represents a person's Higher Form, a person's individualized perfect essence, which descended from God when the individual was created. Looking like a beautiful white angel, the overself is connected to God from the heavens and pours life-giving energy from God into the physical body.

The lessons offered two statements to realize the good in others from a universal standpoint. The first one you say silently for any inharmonious condition: "The I AM Presence of God in me, in (the person's name), and in the Universe now governs this situation." This calls the Higher Form into action and accelerates its ability to help you. It unleashes all the power in the universe when you say it.

The second statement was one to say silently when you meet a person with whom you are having problems: "The I AM Presence of God in me greets the I AM Presence of God in you." This helps the other person, and it helps you to focus on the God-qualities within that person.

I studied and pondered this method to solve the problem with Highpockets. Then I used both statements. Every morning

I would greet him silently with, "The I AM Presence of God in me greets the I AM Presence of God in you."

He actually started smiling. I began to smile! Then Highpockets began taking a few minutes to talk to me about his family. Before this, he had been such a strict worker, he hardly took time out to go to lunch. After a while, Highpockets became even more friendly, and people noticed a difference in him.

As time went by, my feelings toward this man changed from negative to positive. I learned that we truly can change a negative experience into a positive one by using the miracles of the mind. This helped me to conceptualize the workplace as a place in which to grow spiritually.

After I became completely comfortable working with Highpockets, my supervisor told me there was an urgent need to fill a position in the Computer Department. Since the position would be a promotion, I accepted with enthusiasm. One of my new co-workers was on vacation, and I did not have an opportunity to meet her until my first day on the job.

Hilda and I immediately disliked each other. The area of my solar plexus told me: "You are going to have a dreadful time!"

She was another person who was extremely unpopular. In addition, her presence was rather alarming. All I could think of when I looked at her was Elsa Lancaster in the movie, "The Bride of Frankenstein." Her hair was flaming red with corkscrew curls that stuck up in the air, as if an electrical current had been sent through her head.

Whenever we come in contact with a powerful negative, emotional force, a clash can result. Some people might say, "The chemistry is not right" between the two of you. Possibly the person reminds you of someone you do not like. Or if you believe in reincarnation, you might feel that you had encountered the person in a previous lifetime, and the negative memories are reawakening. My feelings for Hilda were so unnerving, I might have been dealing with all of the above.

What would be my creative solution to this problem? I decided to use associative writing to gain clarity, as I had learned from a self-awareness course.

ASSOCIATIVE/FREE FORM WRITING

Free-form writing is like peeling an onion. You remove layers of outer feeling, excess emotional baggage. It is a technique for clearing stress, cleansing negativity, and looking at the basis for certain reactions. You can use this to release emotions, or to vent your feelings when there is no one available with whom you can talk. Use this method to get an answer to a problem by starting out on the top of the page with, "How can I best solve...(fill in the problem)" and wait for what follows. Your superconscious mind often speaks to you from an inner voice that almost sounds like a radio. Or, as some people do, visualize your guardian angel speaking to you.

Putting your feelings on paper is a dynamic morale booster, according to James Pennebaker, Ph.D., professor of psychology at Southern Methodist University in Dallas, Texas. Dr. Pennebaker conducted studies in which he asked students to write for fifteen minutes a day about traumatic experiences. Results showed a more positive attitude after only two weeks of keeping the daily journal, and lasted as long as six months afterward.

Pennebaker reported that students who wrote about thoughts and feelings showed significant improvements in physical health and immune function. They needed fewer doctor visits and felt happier.

It is not necessary to keep a perpetual journal, but only at those times when you are enduring stress over a job loss, divorce or any stress-related situation.

When you find yourself thinking, dreaming or worrying about a problem excessively, I recommend the following:

(1) Set aside twenty minutes each day for writing in a quiet setting where no one will disturb you.
(2) Sit down with paper and pen and write whatever comes to mind. Write without editing. Do not be concerned about grammar or spelling.

(3) Try to describe your problem, along with your deepest
    emotions and thoughts attached to it. Do not show this
    writing to anyone; it is for your eyes only. You might want
    to tear it up afterwards (although when a valuable insight
    comes through, you may want to save it). Or you can create
    your own way to use this form of writing.

Armed with this knowledge, and still thoroughly shaken by
my reactions to Hilda, I took out a sheet of paper and ballpoint
pen. I drew a line down the middle of the sheet. On one side I
wrote the heading, "I like myself when I...." On the other side
of the paper I wrote, "I don't like myself when I...."

I knew that what we like in our self, we like in others; what
we don't like in our self, we don't like in others. This exercise
was intended to reveal what I was facing within myself on a
subconscious level, so that I could understand my reactions to
my co-worker.

One astonishing thing that emerged was that I detested
Hilda's repeating statements to me. On a conscious level, this
had not occurred to me. Then I thought about how she talked to
people as though they had an intelligence quotient lower than
hers. It gave her a feeling of importance; it fed her ego.

When I realized that Hilda's repetition irritated me, I wrote
down that I don't like myself when I repeat a statement. After
thinking long and hard about it, I had to admit that I do repeat
statements when I am not sure I am being heard; when I'm not
certain that people are listening to me, I feel insecure. Aha!

Now I realized that Hilda was hiding feelings of insecurity
behind the confident mask she showed to others. Since people
who are insecure feel the need to pump themselves up, I
received an insight as to why she felt the need to feed her ego at
the expense of others. Her treatment of me was no personal
vendetta; it was simply a habit pattern she had developed out of
her own need. She needed help, but was not about to ask for it.
In spite of that, I was inspired to help her. It was at that time I
found the Angel of Peace Exercise in my library.

ANGEL OF PEACE EXERCISE

The type of personality like Hilda's can be irritating until you understand the reason behind its expressing itself the way it does. Whenever someone causes you to feel stress or irritability, try the following exercise to gain relief, and offer assistance. This is also good to practice at bedtime to bring a refreshing, relaxing sleep that aids in maintaining peace:

(1) When you feel irritated, go to a quiet place where you will be undisturbed. (Fortunately, I could always find a private room such as a women's room or lounge wherever I was employed.) Visualize the Angel of Peace standing above you, pouring a stream of gold-colored healing oil down over your body from head to toe. See your body absorbing this golden healing substance, in the same way a sponge absorbs water. In your conscious mind accept this soothing healing oil as a real happening for at least three minutes, or until you feel its beneficial effect. Remember: thoughts are things. As you see this in your mind's eye, the angel is activated so that the blessings of peace can be bestowed upon you.

(2) Call on your I AM Presence of God to keep this activity sustained so that you will feel continuous peace. Nothing is permanently maintained without the feeling of God's gift of peace.

(3) Another way to apply this exercise is to use it to help another person. We all encounter individuals like Hilda, who are lacking peace in their countenance. When you see that they need help, do a good deed. Instead of reacting with annoyance, try to understand that they may not know how to deal with their stress. This is how you can come to their assistance: Visualize the Angel of Peace standing above that person. See the angel pouring a stream of gold-colored healing oil over the person's body from head to toe. Ask that peace will be sustained for them.

I used the Angel of Peace Exercise to get myself in order, then to help Hilda. It produced remarkable results. Our office became unusually peaceful, and we were able to work as a team and produce outstanding work.

For those who might like a different approach, here is another exercise that I have used myself and have given to students who have felt the need for more harmony or comfort in their office relationships.

HARMONY EXERCISE

By taking fifteen minutes each day, you can train your mind to let only harmony come to you. You can control what you let inside your inner consciousness; you don't have to let anyone inside your inner realm unless they bring peace and harmony. People can talk to your outer self, but they will not have access to your inner self if you set harmony and peace as your ideals and utilize protection with the white light.

Reject all despondent or unhealthy thoughts, which could lead to self-pity and self-centeredness. Instead, visualize the pure loving Light of God pouring into your heart area. This enables you to experience lightness in your mood and enjoy the ability to enter into higher thought realms at will.

Three times a day, turn your attention for five minutes to the energy that causes your heart to beat and is connected to God. This draws you upward and protects you from adverse conditions. Ask that the Holy Spirit's flame of comfort blaze through you. Visualize the flame of comfort as a white water lily bordered in pink. See this flame expand to fill your mind and body and permeate the environment, wherever you are. As you go about your daily activities, affirm that God's nourishing love flows from your heart through every part of your body. Repeat to yourself three times: "All is well ." Think a loving thought such as "God bless you," as you pass individuals during the day. This will bring peace, comfort and many blessings to others and yourself.

We can play a significant role in making our workplace a place of peace instead of a battleground. The more places we can achieve peace, the more we help others to achieve peace and freedom. And the good we do for others we are also doing for ourselves. We are all connected through universal consciousness.

I did not understand the true scope of my encounters with certain individuals and situations, until I came across the following dictation from Zadkiel, Archangel of Transmutation, in the *Daily Meditations* booklet, published by the Ascended Master Teaching Foundation in Mount Shasta, California:

"Do you know that the life within an unkind word comes to you to be REDEEMED AND SET FREE? The life within an unkind look or gesture comes to you—a Priest or Priestess of the Order of Zadkiel--that you might BLESS IT FREE! Do not rebel or feel unjustly treated if circumstances are such that energy qualified with discord comes within the compass of your aura. It comes, because there are few foci in this unascended octave that know how to redeem it, how to raise it, to purify it, to set it free. Where there is a focus of the Sacred Fire, where there is a lifestream who has a knowledge of the Violet Flame, there that energy has an opportunity of being redeemed and returned to the Universal First Cause. Oh, what joy to move in the universe freeing energy, loving it free, and standing in the serene mastery of your own God-hood!"

TREASURE NUMBER NINE: *MAKING PHYSICAL ADJUSTMENTS IN THE WORK ATMOSPHERE*

"Retire often into the silence...Problems that have seemed insoluble will unravel their mysteries in the nook of solitary thoughtfulness."

--Paramahansa Yogananda

Often my students ask: What objects or decorations should I put in my office to create a peaceful atmosphere?

If you work for someone else, you may be limited in how much you can rearrange the office furniture or rooms, and what pictures or photographs you can hang on the walls. You may, however, have certain options that can utilize Feng Shui, the Oriental art of aligning the environment with nature to produce the most desirable results. Feng Shui can show us how to create harmony in the office, as well as the home.

MORE FENG SHUI

In a precious chapter we considered the Chinese tool of Feng Shui, the supervision of laws that govern the earth. The system of Feng Shui deals with the art and science of placement as a direct influence on Vital Force quality. An area that has stagnant energy can easily be transformed into beneficial energy by applying one of the many Feng Shui principles. Here are some Feng Shui pinciples to consider when converting your office environment into a place of peace:

Lighting

Light symbolizes the sun, which is favorable for business atmospheres. Dark rooms or dull lighting oppresses favorable energy. Brilliance in lighting, whether by capturing the sun's rays or by electrical lighting, is essential for harmony in your work surroundings. Since employers know that poor lighting is harmful to the eyes, this is a good reason to lobby for better lighting. All lighting should function sensibly with the environment. As an example, fixtures hanging too low from the ceiling can interfere with activities and harm the occupant's energy.

Plants

Plants are a great way to bring nature into the office. And we can't forget how flowers, or flowering plants add a wonderful scent to the air. Green plants remind us of growth and healing and promote liveliness. If placed in a corner, plants provide even circulation of air and energy, while they take in carbon dioxide and release oxygen. Plants can also act as a buffer against sharp edges around a desk, or any jutting object.

Mirrors

Mirrors are used in Feng Shui to improve the flow of energy and air. If your office has a window facing a river, lake or ocean, you will want to hang a mirror to reflect the water through the window. This draws money energy into the business. Mirrors are often used to deflect negative energy, spirits, or unfavorable wall or room placements, to overcome the visual blocking effects of ill-placed walls, and to draw in positive activities. When someone's back faces the entrance, use a mirror to reflect the image of people coming in the door. That diffuses uneasy feelings about possible intruders, and lessens the risk of being startled—an important precaution.

The placement of mirrors is considered significant. They should not be hung low enough to cut off the top of the head of a person's reflection; that can create headaches. Nor should mirrors be hung too high, which can decrease energy.

CRYSTAL POWER

The legend of King Arthur and his sword, Excalibur, refers to a crystal mounted on the handle of the powerful sword. We have knowledge that North and South American Native Americans carried crystals in their medicine bags for healing purposes. Crystals were also used for meditation and receiving inspiration from the Great Spirit. We know that quartz crystals have been used in watches and electronic technology. So why not use crystals for improving our environment? Although volumes of information could be written on the power and use of these gems, I am only giving a thumbnail sketch of how they have been used in achieving peaceful conditions.

Crystals are energy-containing stones from the earth. Through certain colors and crystalline structures, they can augment our physical, mental, emotional and spiritual natures. We can enhance the energies of a crystal by attuning our conscious mind to them. Selecting and possessing a stone with the positive attributes you need can bring out the best effects for you in your office or home. Following is a list of stones and their beneficial effects. Keep in mind that selecting a personal crystal can involve intuitive response to energies within the stone. Trust your intuition by asking yourself: Which crystal attracts me the most?

Agate: Brings peace, healing, grounding, emotional and physical balance.

Alexandrite: Helps to align mental and emotional functions, as well as spiritual transformation and regeneration.

Amazonite: Soothes the nervous system to bring joy and upliftment; used in ancient Egypt.

Amethyst: Assists with peace, spiritual opening, intuition, self-esteem and sobriety.

Amber: Stabilizes the awakening of kundalini energies and activates the spiritual, altruistic nature.

Aquamarine: Balances physical, emotional, mental aspects; enhances clarity, calm, self-expression.

Adventurine: Promotes healing, prosperity, positive attitude; releases fear.

Azurite: Enhances utilization of oxygen by the body and strengthens blood.

Bloodstone: Balances iron deficiencies, enhances functioning of the heart, spleen, bone marrow and inner guidance.

Celestite: Aids thyroid and throat; helps to adjust to higher states of awareness.

Carnelian: Strengthens creativity, prosperity; used by Egyptians for decoration.

Citrine: Breaks up energy blocks, raises self-esteem, powerful alignment with Higher Self.

Diamond: Best worn with other stones, opens Crown Chakra; master healer.

Dioptase: Tones body, mind and emotions; promotes peace of mind.

Emerald: Enhances dreams, meditation, relaxation; brings victory over conflicts.

Fluorite: Keeps away unwanted people, clears the air of clutter, aids concentration.

Garnet: Lifts self-esteem and will power, calms anger.

Geode: Repels negative people, symbolizes wholeness.

Hematite: Heals, grounds, protects the body.

Herkimer diamond: Enhances dream recall, inner vision, releases stress.

Jade: Generates divine love and wisdom, aids blood and immune system.

Jasper: Helps wearer to lighten up and have fun, improves attitude.

Lapis Lazuli: Stimulates third eye and psychic ability; enhances thought and expression.

Malachite: Helps tissue regeneration, sleep; strengthens glandular system.

Moonstone: Relieves feminine problems, increases intuition, balances emotions.

Obsidian: Wards off negativity, protects against emotional draining; helps to let go of old loves and ways.

Onyx: Balances male/female polarities; enhances self-control and inspiration.

Opal: Stimulates intuition, meditation and the pineal and pituitary glands.

Peridot: Promotes clarity and patience; stimulates clairvoyance.

Pyrite: Attracts money, eases anxiety or frustration.

Quartz Crystal (Clear): Amplifies thought forms, brain functions, reduces negativity in the environment.

Rose quartz: Aids confidence, balances emotions; a love stone.

Ruby: Balances heart and spirit; aids leadership; attracts abundance.

Sapphire: Stimulates telepathy, spiritual receptivity; expands cosmic awareness.

Sardonyx: Bands those together of like natures, links loved ones on an emotional level.

Selenite: Brings positive effect on the brain, power of concentration and clarity.

Smokey Quartz: Excellent for meditation and healing; carries an ultra sound frequency which enables one to develop clairaudience.

Sodalite: Dispels fear and guilt; assists in communication; promotes courage and strength.

Tiger's eye: Assists in separating false desire from need. Softens stubbornness.

Topaz: Balances emotions, promotes understanding, intuition, ability to let go of the past.

Tourmaline: Brings tranquil sleep, peace, spiritual attunement; dispels grief.

Turquoise: Heals, protects against environmental pollutants, increases psychic and communicative skills.

Zircon (Hyacinth): Gives the ability to read images and symbols, a stone for communication with the angels.

How can a crystal help you in the office? Here is a marvelous example. Trixie, the office gossip, was in the habit of visiting my office whenever I was trying to complete an assignment, and I would tell her that I was attempting to meet a deadline. Nonetheless, she would linger beside my desk and bother me with idle chatter. I would ignore her. That did not get my message across, either.

Finally, one morning I was delivering a report to another office where my friend John was working. I was drawn to an attractive mauve geode on his desk. "John," I asked, "where did you get such a pretty paperweight?"

"That's a geode. I got it in the new bookstore. It's supposed to keep bothersome people away from your office."

During my lunch break I ran out and bought one for my desk. I wanted to see if it would help with Trixie. The next day Trixie popped into the office as usual. But this time she appeared to feel uncomfortable and left within minutes. After that, she stayed away. Was I grateful! And so was my supervisor!

Crystals have been honored throughout history by all cultures. They can amplify our thoughts, focus our attention, and radiate vibrations that protect us.

Once you have acquired a crystal from a store or mine, place it in a container with enough sea salt to cover the top of it for forty-eight hours. This will cleanse the crystal of any unwanted vibrations that it may have picked up and restore it to a perfect state for your use.

CRYSTAL EXERCISE:

After you have selected and cleansed your special crystal, hold it in your left hand. Energy flows into the left hand and out the right hand. The right hand can be resting on your lap, or touching a part of your body that may need healing. Take a moment to allow your heart to beat in rhythm with your crystal. You can feel at one with the universe as you hold this crystal. The pulse of the crystal becomes one with your pulsation. Through the crystal, breathe in love and peace from the universe which sparkles with love and peace. As you do this, the crystal illuminates your being with golden white light. You feel a unique peace and stillness. You are moving into the infinite space of the universe. Let yourself become one with the Divine pulsation that ebbs and flows through the universe. Feel Divine Love and Peace flow through your whole being. This allows you to expand and flow upward to experience the joy of love, peace and freedom. You feel a complete oneness, a unity with all there is in the vast universe. When you are ready, let your consciousness flow back into your heart, feeling refreshed and totally at peace.

LAUGHTER TO THE RESCUE

Challenging situations in the business world constantly call for our best performance. But because of human frailties, we do not always perform at our best. This is where humor can come to our rescue.

Susan, a friend of mine, was nervous about giving a talk to 200 executives of a Fortune 500 corporation. As she walked toward the podium, one of her high-heel shoes got caught in a crevice between the rug and the step. On her way down to the floor, her hand tried to brace the fall, dragging a blue tablecloth with her. She quickly recovered by rising from the floor with the tablecloth wrapped around her, saying, "And you thought there wouldn't be entertainment tonight!" Laughter filled the room, and Susan was saved from embarrassment.

The need for humor goes beyond recovering from an unpleasant business episode. In the United States, a sense of humor is regarded as a valuable part of a person's makeup. Whether you are in business, politics, medicine, art, communications or education, a sense of humor is a personality asset that strengthens your image. In addition, humor eases tensions, gives a speaker control, reduces embarrassments, serves as a teaching method, and makes people feel good.

Research pioneers, such as William F. Fry, Jr., emeritus professor of clinical psychiatry at Stanford University, report that laughter can reduce pain and stress, stimulate mental functions, and improve the immune system. One study showed marked increases of interferon-gamma, which fights viruses and regulates cell growth, in a group of men who watched a humorous video for an hour. The effect of this hormone remained with them for as much as twelve hours later.

Doctors are realizing more and more that if we laugh a little each day, it can do spectacular things for our health. A book that was on the New York Times bestseller list, *Anatomy of an Illness as Perceived by the Patient* by Norman Cousins, specifies laughter as one of the components that cured him of a serious disease of the connective tissue. For me, this book was an eye-opener as his innovative approach to disease unfolded. He found that laughter had a pain-killing effect similar to the hormone, endorphin, released by the brain during exercise.

Cousins found that ten minutes of robust belly laughter allowed him to sleep for two hours without pain. When the pain-killing effect wore off, he would watch Marx Brothers movies, or read hilarious books that would send him into a spin of laughter again. Consequently, this enabled him to enjoy a few more hours of pain-free sleep without drugs and unwanted side-effects.

My uncle Joe was always a joy to be around. Often certain events will trigger the memory of one of his jokes and make me giggle. I would like to seal this chapter by sharing one of his gems:

A man went to the doctor for a routine examination.

Doctor: You're in good shape for a man of 63.

Patient: Who said I was 63?

Doctor: Well, that is what I thought I saw on your records.

Patient: I'm 83.

Doctor: You're in excellent shape for a man of 83! How long did your father live?

Patient: Who said my father died? He's 103.

Doctor: Then how long did your grandfather live?

Patient: Who said my grandfather died? He's 123 and he's getting married!

Doctor: I can't imagine why a man of 123 would want to get married.

Patient: Who said he wants to get married?

Whether you are a person who has to deal with stress at work, or someone who wants to strengthen your public image, or even your immune system, employ the best kind of medicine. Use laughter. Look for the seed of humor in every situation.

Watch how it will lighten your day, as you roll on billows of laughter and spread feelings of joy in the world.

SECTION SUMMARY

Every day we see examples of individuals who are spiritual in their home and in their private lives. But then they slip into a different skin—more worldly, competitive—as they enter the business arena. This is not the way to achieve an elevated consciousness, nor the way to achieve mastery of our physical world.

Once you expand your perspective of life, it cannot apply only to some areas. For instance, if you accept the oneness of all human beings and feel connected on a universal level, then you cannot use cutthroat techniques against a competitor in the marketplace. You would understand that hurting another being will only hurt yourself later on.

One method of finding peace in stressful situations, or in dealing with difficult co-workers is to bring out their best, not by looking at what they are expressing, but by focusing on and silently affirming their I AM Presence of God. In India, enlightened individuals greet each other by putting their hands together as if in prayer, bowing their head and saying, "Namaste." It means "I greet the Divinity within you. I honor the place in you which is of love, light and peace. When you are in that place in you, and I am in that place in me, we are one."

A second method to relieve stress and get to the root of a problem involves Associative/Free-form writing. Valuable insights can come through this practice.

Other methods to apply can be the Angel of Peace Exercise to help both you and the other person, the Harmony Exercise and laughter.

Feng Shui, the Chinese art of placement, can be advantageous by bringing harmony into the office, as well as the home, with careful alignment with nature. Certain objects can induce a peaceful atmosphere: lighting, plants, mirrors and crystals.

We are working with the Universal Law of Cause and Effect in the above situations: As you sow, you shall reap; what you expect, you will receive; like attracts like; nothing happens by chance; what goes around, comes around; or he that would have peace, must make peace with self and others.

As this section draws to a close, I commend to you my friend, Elizabeth. She lives in England and is ninety-three as of this writing. No one can believe her age because of the physical and mental health that she enjoys. Elizabeth, who had set her feet on the spiritual path several years ago, is a living example that you can rise above the limitations of age when you find peace through the pearls of knowledge in our treasure chest.

EPILOGUE: *A NEW ERA*

"Birth of the White Buffalo Calf lets us know we are at a crossroads—either return to balance or face global disaster. It's our duty to return to sacred places and pray for world peace—if we do not do this, our children will suffer."

--Chief Arvol Looking Horse,
Lakota-Dakota-Nakota Nation, 19th Generation
Keeper of the Sacred White Buffalo Calf Pipe

On August 20, 1994, a white buffalo calf was born on a farm in Janesville, Wisconsin. The blessed event was announced on national news broadcasts that night, and the animal's photograph was featured in newspapers around the United States. People traveled thousands of miles to honor the event. Why? Because the odds of this phenomenon happening are one in a million, and, according to a Lakota Sioux legend, she signals the return of a Native American goddess.

The legend says that a goddess appeared before the starving Plains Indians. She taught them many spiritual truths, told them about buffalo, and became known as White Buffalo Woman. She brought the original sacred pipe, so that by smoking it, the people could become more strong, prosperous, reverent and reach the Great Spirit.

White Buffalo Woman instructed the people on the meaning of the sacred pipe ceremony: The bowl of the pipe holds the tobacco. The stem of the pipe unites with the bowl, representing the union of male and female to produce life. This union is symbolic of our connection to the energy of the Great Spirit. The community was invited to enter into the pipe and share its smoke, symbolizing prayer and praise to the Great Spirit. This sacred act had a cleansing, purifying effect on the participants.

It became time for White Buffalo Woman to leave, but she promised to return in the form of a white buffalo to herald an era of spiritual awakening on Earth, a time of peace, unity and the end of racial strife. Then she turned herself into a white buffalo calf and disappeared. After that, herds of buffalo arrived to provide food and clothing for the people.

In many Indian traditions, the white buffalo is the most sacred of all animals. Its presence is an omen that prayers are being heard and that prophecy is being fulfilled. The Native Americans believe that the birth of the white buffalo calf is the fulfillment of the Lakota Sioux legend and encouragement that the time has come for spiritual awakening and peace. Other Native Americans believe that more evidence of this will unfold after the turn of the new millennium.

Meanwhile, the owners of the farm in Janesville, Wisconsin, have undergone a spiritual renewal from witnessing visitors of all races and creeds drawn to the phenomenal buffalo. One unusual observation has been the changing of the buffalo's color to represent the races of visitors. For example, while the calf was growing, her coat changed into the colors of red, brown, yellow, then back to white.

Mayan teachings concur with predictions of a worldwide shift in consciousness. Native American Hunbatz-Men, called Day Keeper of Mayan wisdom and recognized as the foremost interpreter of the Mayan calendar, predicted enormous changes from March 21, 1995, onward. Hunbatz-Men and his ancestors have safeguarded the secrets of Mayan science and religion during the past five hundred years. According to Mayan teachings, the time has come for the Light to be activated in each person.

An honored shaman in the Los Angeles, California area, Shrinat Devi, was inspired to gather a group of powerful healers for February 19, and 20, 2000 at a special site in the desert near Giant Rock to pray and meditate. It was prophesied that the earth was about to react with a violent upheaval and special prayer was necessary. If Mother Earth accepted their special prayers, then Giant Rock would crack at the side, thereby relieving the pressure that could cause earthquakes. If the prayers were not accepted, then Giant Rock would split straight down the middle.

At 8:20 a.m., February 21, a large rock fell off from the boulder of Giant Rock, considered to be the largest boulder of the world. One-third of the rock had split, on the side instead of the middle, interpreted by Shrinat Devi to mean that Mother earth had opened her arms, cracking open her heart for all to see. Their prayers were answered. The rock had not split in half.

Later, at the home of Shrinat Devi, lightning struck, sending light in a north/south direction, followed by a strike in an east/west direction. This was witnessed by four people. Shrinat Devi said that this was an omen that the Mother had supported the completion of the prayers and a shift is taking place. We stand at the threshold of an opportunity to discover the Peace and Compassion of the Divine within ourselves—we are going through a transformation. Spirit asks that we purify ourselves because we are entering a time when we have to let go of pretense and live the real truth.

The book, *You are Becoming a Galactic Human* by Virginia Essene and Sheldon Nidle, has a provocative message. It states that the Solar System is preparing to enter a region of light referred to as the **Photon Belt** and a higher dimension. As a part of the preparation and transit through the Photon Belt, uncanny happenings such as the malfunction of electricity and a period of darkness are indicated. Interestingly, this prophecy is similar to the Three Days of Darkness Prophecy given by Our Blessed Mother to holy people such as Padre Pio (Capuchin priest, Italy), the children at Fatima, and at Medjugorje, Yugoslavia.

When the Solar System and Earth move into a higher dimension, as described in *You are Becoming a Galactic Human,* it will create a tremendous infusion of light energy, transformation of our DNA and chakra centers, and a new awareness in the collective consciousness of humanity.

Are we entering a time of higher consciousness, awareness, and dimension? And what does that mean, anyway?

We are getting ready to enter a brand new epoch. The Earth is positioning itself to enter a higher dimension than the one it now occupies. The inhabitants of our planet are being prepared for entering a higher consciousness...not because the White Buffalo appeared...not because of the Mayan predictions, but because the adherence to spiritual principles is necessary for the survival and advancement of the human race. Preparing for a shift in consciousness involves a change in values, perspective and life focus.

You don't have to be a guru from India to be aware that changes are occurring on our planet and within humanity. The White Buffalo and the Mayan Return are merely two signals that the Universe is sending us about a new era.

Other signs of changes are all around us. Books on angels flood the market with stories of how people were conscious of angels helping them. (According to esoteric studies, one sign of the new golden age is angels working closely with humanity.) Students of higher consciousness are adding their positive vibrations to the equation, such as the world peace movement where thousands set an appointed time to pray and meditate on world peace. The attendance at New Thought and Unity churches continues to increase. More and more people are meditating, forming study groups and sharing inspirational information. Celebrities involved are Marianne Williamson, who bases her work on the classic, *A Course in Miracles*, and Louise Hay, whose thrust is self-healing.

Individuals who have not been a part of society's growing interest in metaphysics and spirituality might feel overwhelmed, confused, frightened or anxious—and certain signs of the approaching epoch can cause discomfort. For example, time has speeded up; it is more difficult for people to get things done in the same time frame as before. And weather patterns are erratic. Strange physical symptoms appear in the body for which there is no explanation upon undergoing physical exams. In many cases it is a reflection of the change in the DNA structure.

The time coding of the Great Pyramid of Egypt indicates a spiritual eruption that will bring humanity to closer spiritual and material perfection. According to the Great Pyramid, the date for the Kingdom of Heaven to begin to manifest on earth was February 21, 1999. While it has not become materially obvious to us, this is causing a change of energy in the earth through its major chakra centers, such as Giza, Egypt, Stonehenge, England, and Diamond Head, Hawaii. The DNA structure of humanity is moving from a seven chakra energy system to a twelve chakra system. We are shifting from 46 base pairs of DNA to 48 base pairs. Some of this can be seen in the so-called Indigo Children. These are children who reveal an unusual set of psychological attributes, displaying an undocumented behavior pattern which is baffling parents, doctors and teachers.

Most people do not like change; they fear the unexpected. We cannot, however, have a better world while conditions remain as they are. The veil has to be removed from the eyes of humanity, just as the midwife had to remove the veil from Dora's eyes so that she could see. This enabled Dora to have the vision to see beyond the world of appearance into a world of finer substance. Some upheaval cannot be avoided. Think of what happens when you clean a house. Furniture and objects have to be moved so the dirt can be swept away, and the house looks in disarray as part of the process. But after the cleaning is done, order returns.

Can you picture a cleaner, more beautiful world? As co-creators with God of our earthly experience, we are being asked to take part in the cleansing of our existence. This starts with a new, positive vision, a more spiritually-centered life, and an improved home and office atmosphere. Our physical environment and our relationships need the necessary adjustments to reflect peace and love. Whatever we give out, comes back to us.

The following quote is taken from the book on *Cosmic Law, Lesson Four,* of a series of twenty-one lessons, published by the Ascended Master Teaching Foundation of Mount Shasta, California:

"Harmony, an action of divine love, requires the continuous pouring forth of kindly feelings of good will to each other. To be in a continuous state of harmony, we need to look to the God-Presence I AM and the Ascended Host of Light for guidance, protection, happiness and PEACE! Let each of us say

and FEEL: 'God grant us PEACE, and LET IT BEGIN WITH ME!' "

The challenges humanity faces are being brought to the forefront to be transmuted. The problems are not to make us afraid, but to make us more determined to hasten the change for a better society and planet. Usually human beings need a crisis to move them into action. Are we going to wait for an emergency to awaken us, or are we going to take positive steps before it is too late? We have to help ourselves, then do what we can to assist others and the environment.

What is being brought to the forefront to change or transmute in your life? What area of your life needs healing? Do you have an addiction or bad habit that is holding back your progress to the finer things in life? Do you have to overcome something alone? No. We are never alone. One of our many gifts of assistance from God was brought to our attention by Jesus. Speaking to his disciples, He said: "But I speak the truth to you; it is expedient for you that I go away. For if I do not go, the Comforter will not come to you; but if I go I will send him to you." (John 16:7)

Jesus was speaking about the Holy Spirit, the nurturing aspect of God, symbolized as a white dove, representing peace. The Comforter was sent for us, as well as for the apostles. Jesus knew we would need help after he left. The Comforter is still active two thousand years later, bringing us the Truth and new life in the Holy Spirit of God. Whatever we need to complete, no matter how overwhelming it may seem, we can call on the Holy Spirit and receive the comfort of heaven.

How do we call upon the Comforter to help us put our house in order or to receive special counsel? One way is through the prayer, "Come, Holy Spirit, fill the hearts of thy faithful and enkindle in them the fire of Divine Love. Send forth Thy Spirit, and they shall be created, and Thou shalt renew the face of the earth."

Psalm 91:1 says, "He that dwelleth in the secret place of the Most High" may find peace and protection. This is achieved through meditation, contemplation and by realizing that every soul needs to live the commandment: To love God with all your heart, mind and soul, and your neighbor as your self. When we nurture ourselves and others without seeking reward, then we become lovable, and the reward of being loved will find us.

One problem I see today is that people do not love themselves enough. This is due to old tapes from the past that we play over in our minds—insecurities ingrained by trying to live up to someone else's erroneous idea of what we should be. Perhaps a new commandment is called for: Thou shalt love thyself better. The beating up on ourselves must go, be transmuted, so that we can learn who we truly are—divine beings. Once we can express the divinity within ourselves, others will see the beauty that is not physical, but spiritual, and this helps them to see it in themselves. We can't destroy the lower self, the ego, the rebellious child within. But we can transmute it with the violet flame, then love it free, blazing it with the pink flame of divine love.

By quieting the mind through prayer, meditation, contemplation and saying the decrees, you are no longer vulnerable to external influences. You can train yourself to be so centered that you can shut out noise, create light, and experience healing miracles.

In order to experience miracles, we need to get rid of our *limited* expectations and behavior patterns that followed us into adulthood based on negative feedback from others. If we can get rid of the limited beliefs, which led us down the yellow brick road to the Wizard of Oz (who turned out to be a fake), we can get on the path of enlightenment leading to perfection.

William James (1842—1910), referred to as the father of modern psychology and noted scientist of Harvard University, said that humans live too much within self-imposed limits. He foresaw that these limits would recede—as soon as we understood the natural drive of the mind and body toward perfectibility and regeneration. Allowing this drive to manifest will be the finest exercise toward humanity's freedom.

I would like to share a special message that I received in meditation. This is for you who are called to the path of enlightenment:

Let your mind be open as lilies in the water. There are eight lilies representing eight times each day most favorable for meditation: sunrise, 9:00 a.m., noon, 3:00 p.m., 6:00 p.m., sunset, 9:00 p.m. and midnight. The wind moves the water lilies along the pond. The wind represents the Holy Spirit, the breath of life. It carries what you need for growth. Growth is the natural order of life. All forms of consciousness are in a continual process of change and growth. You may choose to evolve slowly with the masses or quicken your evolution.

The day is coming when you will know what lies before you. The earth is changing and has need of those who understand what is taking place. The Holy Spirit brings the gift of understanding and what needs to be done. You have a spiritual purpose, a mission that is beautiful. Know that it will bear fruit. No one is on the earth without a soul purpose. These days are for learning. Dwell on this: Happy are those who wait on the Lord.

The Lord seems slow in delivering to you what you have longed for. This is a testing, and you can pass the test. Look forward to the future in faith, knowing that there will manifest a new way of seeing the world and the heavens. You are not forsaken, and soon you will understand this. "Soon" has been promised to you for a long time, just as the people in biblical days waited for the coming of the Messiah. These people waited with hope, faith and patience. Hope, faith and patience are needed to pass the test of waiting. Faith is measured by patience.

You need to protect yourself from all that would bring harm or disturb you by realizing that you are enveloped in an impenetrable armor of love and light, and evil cannot reach into this.

Find something good in your life to be happy about now, for tomorrow will bring something entirely different.

Therefore, rejoice in the Lord always, knowing that you are experiencing His good, even though it may not appear to be that way.

Practice what the sacred teachings call "listening grace." Allow time to pray and hear the Holy Spirit. If you are not open to the guidance of the Holy Spirit, it will go on to someone else. And someone else will get the opportunity for which you have waited. Many individuals have lost grand opportunities by not allowing time for <u>listening grace.</u>

Remember that you are living in a world of appearances and need to see beyond the surface of things. Do not be fooled by how a matter may seem at first. Magicians rely on tricks that the human eye can miss. When you are puzzled, take a moment to go within. Ask the Holy Spirit to show you the truth. It is through the Holy Spirit's gift of discernment that you will know the truth.

Discernment is the testing of what is true and untrue. Discernment <u>in relation to people:</u> By their fruits you will know them. Look closely at the individual who may be trying to impress you, or persuade you to do something. Are they manifesting something good in their lives? Do they serve or help others? Discernment <u>in relation to oneself:</u> Discernment is the deep evaluation of one's desires. Be honest with yourself. Do your desires serve God and others, or do they serve only self and become self-destructive? In meditation you will hear two voices: the lower self (the ego) and the higher self. If the voice sounds contradictory, hurried, appealing to the ego with false pride, or doubtful, it is the voice of the lower self. If it is the still, small voice that speaks of love, peace, confidence and patience, it is the higher self. You will come to know the higher voice because deep inside, you will know when it feels right, without doubt. <u>Discernment in relation to God's will:</u> Someone may say it is God's will to do thus and so. If you are unsure, ask these questions. Is it good for the community? Is it a value found in the Holy Scriptures? Does it manifest love?

The cries from Earth call for comfort from pain, loneliness, uncertainty, unhappiness and disappointment. The comforting presence of the Holy Spirit is God's answer to this heart call. Learn to abide in that presence through the steps that I have outlined.

On the day of Pentecost, the disciples of Jesus, feeling hopeless and confused by all that had taken place, knelt and prayed together to find strength, hope and the way of their spiritual mission. At that moment the Holy Spirit, that which was promised, descended upon each head in the form of a flame. The promise of the Comforter was not reserved for the disciples, but for all of humanity thereafter. The blessing was poured out so that all of humanity could partake of the light brought by Jesus. There was a raising of vibration never before felt upon the earth. A new life was born within the disciples.

Since that day of Pentecost, humanity has experienced many new blessings and miracles from the Holy Spirit. And these will continue to even a greater scope as humanity awakens to its true spiritual purpose. This can happen through knowledge of the Comforter within, and a raising of vibration to where all hatred and negative conditions are transmuted into love and positive conditions. What we cannot do alone, the Holy Spirit can do through us, guiding us to Spiritual Freedom as Earth becomes Freedom's Holy Star.

Jeanette, one of my students, told me how the Holy Spirit worked through her when she prayed for the right words to say to her relatives who were causing her problems. She had said her prayer before their meeting. When it was time to speak to them, words came out of her mouth, but she can not remember what she said. "All I know," Jeanette said, "is that they have not bothered me since."

Do we understand that the physical body is a vehicle which carries the spark of God within, an individualized portion of God, that is going through earthly experiences to help us learn and grow on our return to the Godhead? Our destiny is to manifest a fullness of love and God-being not experienced prior to this time.

The visitation experience in California was one of those moments in my life that served as a journey post. (I am referring to my experience in Treasure Number Three.) It took one of life's storms for me to see the Holy Spirit of God—His light, His love, His caring, through the form of Mother Mary. After that I could never be the same. The storm of suffering now seems like a small price to pay for a glimpse of God.

Knowledge is a key that unlocks hidden treasures of wisdom which lie within the soul. Wisdom is also awakened by the whisper of the Comforter.

Perhaps you have felt the Comforter very near. But you may not have been able to hear the knock or open the door—only because your tools of intuition were not sharpened.

Now you have a key—the remembrance of who you truly are. You are a Divine Son/Daughter of God, a temporary traveler on the earth plane, awaiting the fulfillment of your soul purpose so that you can return to a higher realm. This remembrance helps you reconnect to the Kingdom of Heaven within. The door opens to the awareness of your Higher Self, your connection to God. The door opens to *El Dorado*, "The Golden One." This awareness enables the Higher Self to express through you in the most positive way. When Jesus said that the truth shall set you free, it was the realization of the truth of the oneness with God that he was talking about.

We are entering a spiritual age, which will be second to nothing ever experienced before. Get ready to accept the Divine Blessings pouring over the Earth. Prepare yourself for release into Spiritual Freedom.

May you be empowered with the nourishing goodness of the Holy Spirit of God. May you walk in His Light, live on in His Love, and be enfolded in His Peace. May you experience that Joy which no person, no circumstance, can take from you. Then you will be able to become a presence of comfort within yourself and to your neighbor. And the treasures of peace that surpass all understanding will be yours.

RECOMMENDED READING

Ayscough, Florence. <u>A Chinese Mirror</u>. Boston: Houghton Mifflin, 1925.

Bailey, Alice. <u>Initiation, Human and Solar</u>. New York: Lucis Publishing Company, 1922.

Butler, W. E. <u>How to Develop Clairvoyance</u>. London: The Aquarian Press, 1968.

Coit, Lee. <u>Listening: How to Increase Awareness of Your Inner Guide</u>. Wildomar, California: KNI, Inc., 1985.

Cousins, Norman. Anatomy of an Illness. New York: W.W. Norton and Co., 1979.

Davis, John and Rice, Naomi. <u>Messiah and the Second Coming.</u> Michigan: Coptic Press, 1982.

DeBary, William Theodore, ed. <u>Sources of Chinese Tradition</u>. 3 vols. New York and London: Columbia University Press 1970.

Essene, Virginia and Nidle, Sheldon. <u>You Are Becoming a Galactic Human</u>. Santa Clara, CA: S.E.E. Publishing Company, 1994.

Gewurz, Elias. <u>The Hidden Treasures of the Ancient Qabalah.</u> Desplaines, Illinois: Yoga Publication Socoety, 1918.

Luk, A.D.K.. <u>Law of Life</u>, 2 vols. Oklahoma City: A.D.K. Luk Publishing, 1959.

McGarey, Gladys and William. <u>There Will Your Heart Be Also</u>. New York: Warner Books, 1976.

Saso, Michael. <u>Taoism and the Rite of Cosmic Renewal</u>. Pullman, Washington: Washington State University Press, 1972.

Sechrist, Elsie. <u>Dreams, Your Magic Mirror</u>. New York: Dell Publishing Company, 1968.

Scully, Nicki. <u>The Golden Cauldron</u>. Santa Fe, New Mexico: Bear & Company, 1991.

Schroeder, Werner. <u>Man, His Origin, History and Destiny</u>. Mount Shasta, California: Ascended Master Teaching Foundation, 1984.

Sherrow, Victoria. <u>Watson and Crick: Decoding the Secrets of DNA</u>. Woodbridge, Connecticut: Blackbirch Press, 1995.

Spalding, Baird T. Life and Teachings of the Masters of the Far East, 5 vols. Los Angeles: Devorss & Company, 1924.

Woolf, Virginia. A Room of One's Own. New York and London: Harcourt Brace and World, 1957.

ABOUT THE AUTHOR

Mary Gemming is a teacher and minister who has utilized her intuitive skills to help others sustain peace and harmony to manifest a more positive life since 1978 in New York State and Florida.